Are Filter Bubbles Real?

Digital Futures Series

Are Filter Bubbles Real?

AXEL BRUNS

polity

The right of Axel Bruns to be identified as Author of this Work has been asserted in accordance with the UK Copyright, Designs and Patents Act 1988.

First published in 2019 by Polity Press

Polity Press
65 Bridge Street
Cambridge CB2 1UR, UK

Polity Press
101 Station Landing
Suite 300
Medford, MA 02155, USA

ISBN-13: 978-1-5095-3644-3
ISBN-13: 978-1-5095-3645-0(pb)

A catalogue record for this book is available from the British Library.

Typeset in 11 on 15 Adobe Garamond by
Servis Filmsetting Ltd, Stockport, Cheshire
Printed and bound in Great Britain by TJ International Ltd

The publisher has used its best endeavours to ensure that the URLs for external websites referred to in this book are correct and active at the time of going to press. However, the publisher has no responsibility for the websites and can make no guarantee that a site will remain live or that the content is or will remain appropriate.

Every effort has been made to trace all copyright holders, but if any have been overlooked the publisher will be pleased to include any necessary credits in any subsequent reprint or edition.

For further information on Polity, visit our website: politybooks.com *v*

This book emerged as an unexpected companion to my 2018 monograph *Gatewatching and News Curation: Journalism, Social Media, and the Public Sphere*. As I wrote that book, it became increasingly clear how much we are hampered, misled, and distracted from more important questions by the metaphors of echo chambers and filter bubbles that are no longer fit for purpose, and probably never were. From my conversations at the Association of Internet Researchers, International Communication Association, Social Media & Society, and Future of Journalism conferences, I know that many of my colleagues feel the same.

If, like me, you're fed up with these vague concepts, based on little more evidence than hunches and anecdotes, this book is for you; if you think that there's still some value in using them, I hope I am at least able to introduce some more specific definitions and empirical rigour into the debate. In either case, perhaps I will convince you that the debate about these information cocoons distracts us from more critical questions at present.

"We are hampered, misled, and distracted from more important questions by the metaphors of echo chambers and filter bubbles that are no longer fit for purpose."

Acknowledgements

My sincere thanks to the many colleagues with whom I've discussed the themes of this book – in particular, my colleagues in the Digital Media Research Centre at Queensland University of Technology. Many thanks also to Mary Savigar at Polity for a number of stimulating discussions about the shape of the book. My research was supported by the Australian Research Council Future Fellowship project *Understanding Intermedia Information Flows in the Australian Online Public Sphere*, Discovery project *Journalism beyond the Crisis: Emerging Forms, Practices and Uses*, and LIEF project *TrISMA: Tracking Infrastructure for Social Media in Australia*.

ONE

Introduction:
More than a Buzzword?

As they leave the White House, outgoing US Presidents reflect on their experience. In 1961, Dwight D. Eisenhower used his final television address to warn of the 'grave implications' of the powerful military-industrial complex that – as a former World War Two general and Supreme Commander of NATO – he had himself helped to create. Only an 'alert and knowledgeable citizenry' could act as a corrective and control to the 'unwarranted influence' of the military-industrial complex (1961: 2–3); though the Cold War has ended, his warning resonates still.

Barack Obama's farewell speech in Chicago on 10 January 2017 warned of a different danger, similarly requiring attention from an alert and knowledgeable public: amidst increasingly heated and uncivil political discourse, he suggested, 'for too many of us it's become safer to retreat into our own bubbles, whether in our neighbourhoods, or on college campuses, or places of worship, or especially our social media feeds, surrounded by people who look like us and share the same political outlook and never challenge our assumptions' (Obama 2017: n.p.). Like Eisenhower, Obama should know a good deal about this topic: after all, with his own online community site *my.barackobama.com* and later with mainstream platforms such as *Facebook* and *Twitter*, he is widely recognised as the first US President to successfully use social media in election campaigning.

Obama's concerns are far from new, however. Under labels such as 'echo chambers' and 'filter bubbles', they are held responsible for a broad variety of social and political problems. Social media – and the content filtering and recommendation algorithms they rely on – have been identified as one reason that such phenomena have emerged; before them, search engines and the overall multiplication, fragmentation, and personalisation of available media sources in the Internet age were also highlighted as contributing factors. Put simply, the argument goes, if we all disappear into our different information cocoons, where we only ever encounter like-minded others and are served a highly selective media and information diet, then society fragments. Worse still, because it requires a well-informed citizenry and cross-ideological dialogue to reach a broadly supported consensus about the future direction of the state, democracy itself falters.

This book addresses these concerns and reviews the evidence for and against echo chambers and filter bubbles (in search, social media, and beyond). Ultimately, it argues that such fears about the societal effects of disconnected informational spaces, and about the role of new media technologies in their creation, only divert our attention from the much more critical question of what drives the increasing polarisation and hyperpartisanship in many established and emerging democracies.

Obama's warning followed Donald Trump's surprise victory in the US presidential election in November 2016; it mirrors similar concerns after the UK's Brexit referendum in June 2016, and other apparently unexpected wins for populist causes and candidates, despite widespread coverage of their personal and policy flaws. Politicians, journalists, and scholars who support the echo chamber or filter bubble thesis suggest that, with online and social media as the key sources of information for an ever-growing percentage of the public, it became possible for citizens to be locked into 'ideological filter bubbles that lacked cross-cutting information' (Groshek and Koc-Michalska 2017: 1390). Brexit supporters might never have seen the warnings of the disastrous economic, social, and political consequences of exiting the European Union; Trump followers might not have encountered reports of the candidate's personal flaws or the campaign's collusion with foreign powers.

Away from these momentous occasions, echo chambers and filter bubbles are also held responsible for the emergence of many more communities that espouse contrarian and counterfactual perspectives and ideologies. These include comparatively harmless conspiracy theorists compiling evidence of alien visitations; groups of agitators who steadfastly deny the reality of anthropogenic climate change or the benefits of population-wide vaccination; and extremists preaching racism, homophobia, and religious intolerance. The argument is that echo chambers enable these groups to reinforce their views by connecting with like-minded others, and that filter bubbles shield them from encountering contrary perspectives.

Such disconnection from and ignorance of alternative perspectives is said to result from a combination of individual choice, in selecting the news sources to consult or the social media accounts to follow, and the algorithmic shaping of such choices, as search engines, news portals, and social media platforms highlight and recommend some sources over others. As platform algorithms learn from users' choices, and users make those choices predominantly from the options promoted by the algorithms, a self-reinforcing feedback loop gradually curtails choice to an increasingly narrow and homogeneous set of options (Bozdag and van den Hoven 2015: 252). Such processes are also susceptible to interference from malicious actors: the operators of the mis- and disinformation campaigns described by the problematic label 'fake news' seek to manipulate and exploit the logic of social media platforms and their content recommendation algorithms to give their own, fabricated material more prominence than higher-quality content from reputable sources (Woolley and Howard 2017: 6).

Yet even in the absence of deliberate misinformation campaigns, the algorithmic shaping of information streams is problematic. The algorithms follow opaque and non-transparent decision-making processes whose effects are rarely articulated clearly to the user: why does *Google Search* or *Google News* present a certain set of results for a given search term, for example? Why does the *Facebook* newsfeed highlight certain posts from the user's network and hide others? Why does *Twitter* recommend specific accounts to follow or trending hashtags to explore? These selections build on the individual user's and the broader userbase's actions, but exactly how they are incorporated into the algorithm's logic remains unknown. At worst, by highlighting the most popular content and thereby making it even more widely visible, the algorithm encourages a form of unconstrained majority rule, where only already popular accounts and content can ever cut through to a wider audience. Amidst a self-perpetuating and even self-amplifying stream of majority voices, minority views are overwhelmed and silenced, and genuinely open public debate between nuanced and diverse perspectives is rendered impossible (Bozdag and van den Hoven 2015: 254).

These, in brief, are the key concerns of those who worry about the impact of echo chambers and filter bubbles; we will explore them in more detail in the following chapters. But are these 'frequent lamentations' (Guess 2016: 2) warranted? Is there actual empirical evidence for the existence of such ideological cocoons? Are there other explanations for increasing political fragmentation?

These fears emerged at a time of considerable political upheaval, but also of substantial change in the way news is produced, disseminated, and used. The era of news as 'a fairly stable product', delivered via print or broadcast, is almost over (Nielsen 2016: 112). Institutional and technological disruption has always coincided with significant moral panics about what an as yet only imperfectly formed future might hold: the printing press, telegraph, radio, TV, and the early Web each saw similar moral panics about their impact on how citizens might reliably inform themselves about the news (or else be manipulated by populists and demagogues).

This does not mean such fears should be dismissed immediately: the printing press did play an important role in mobilising the public during the American revolution, for example, just as radio did in recruiting popular support for the fascist regimes of the 1930s. Yet these developments did not result inevitably from the technologies themselves, but from how they were utilised by political actors: for good or evil, to reject colonial masters or claim mastery over others, human agency in deploying these technologies channelled their potential power. A moral panic about social media in themselves, then, independent of how and by whom they are used, is no more warranted than one about TV, radio, or the printing press. We would fall for technological determinism: a belief that social media, however platforms might be designed and however citizens might use them, inevitably promote echo chambers and filter bubbles. As we will see, there is no evidence to support such an argument (O'Hara and Stevens 2015: 409). We cannot absolve ourselves from the mess we are in by simply blaming technology.

Because they tap into apparently common-sense understandings of our world, however, moral panics are deeply persuasive, and echo chamber and filter bubble concepts have therefore been accepted widely (often rather unquestioningly) in scholarly and popular literature. In particular, even while ramping up their own social media offerings, mainstream news media have gladly accepted the idea of social media as echo chambers because it enables them to claim that, compared to these new competitors for the attention of news audiences, only the carefully researched and edited news published by established news outlets offers a balanced news diet that penetrates the cocoon. Similarly, for political operatives, the filter bubble has become a handy slur: just as President Trump will dismiss any critical reporting as 'fake news', so can politicians now accuse their opponents of 'living in a filter bubble', out of touch with 'ordinary people'.

Such use and abuse of these concepts for political point-scoring is possible because, despite their apparently intuitive meanings, 'echo chamber' and 'filter bubble' have remained very poorly defined. Even scholarly work tends to use these terms interchangeably (e.g. Graham and Ackland 2017: 190) rather than attempting to distinguish the two. Such conceptual confusion creates considerable variation in how these

"We cannot absolve ourselves from the mess we are in by simply blaming technology."

terms are understood in the research, and frustrates the search for hard evidence of their existence. Even the authors who introduced and popularised these terms, Cass Sunstein ('echo chambers') and Eli Pariser ('filter bubbles'), generally fail to provide clear definitions or to outline concrete methodological approaches for detecting them. As chapter 2 shows in more detail, their early contributions draw largely on hypothetical thought experiments or personal anecdotes, and envisage their deleterious consequences without checking such dark visions against established knowledge about the preferences and behaviours of actual users.

Echo chambers, for instance, would be most effective if their inhabitants use them as the *only* source of information, but this seems highly improbable in the massively multi-channel environment of the contemporary mediasphere (Dubois and Blank 2018a, 2018b). Filter bubbles, meanwhile, are premised on 'who one's friends are . . .: If you have only liberal friends, you're going to see a dramatic reduction in conservative news' (Pariser 2015: n.p.). Yet making friends purely on the basis of political leaning seems unlikely for most people. In general, both concepts assign far too much importance to the role of politics in ordinary people's lives: the selection of friends and followers in social media based on *political* compatibility is outweighed by friendship, professional, entertainment and other considerations that have little to do with politics in the narrow sense. In discussing ideological cocoons, we must not forget that the vast majority of users are not on social media primarily to talk politics.

The empirical work on echo chambers and filter bubbles that does exist suffers from further limitations, which we will explore in chapters 3 and 4. It is not sufficient to prove that groups on a single social media platform, or even within a specific space within that platform – a *Facebook* group or *Twitter* hashtag, for example – appear to constitute an echo chamber or filter bubble, disconnected from the wider world outside. Such studies do not address 'the actual experiences of individuals' (Dubois and Blank 2018b: n.p.), because real users do not normally participate only within a single social media space, or engage only with a single platform within the overall mediasphere. A user who participates in an apparent echo chamber on *Facebook* while consuming a broad diet of mainstream news through other channels does not exist in an information cocoon, however ideologically homogeneous their *Facebook* community might be.

Indeed, for users who generally maintain a diverse media diet through other channels, the increased personalisation and filtering available in online and social media can be 'empowering' (Zuiderveen Borgesius et al. 2016: 5): it provides them with increased autonomy over their news consumption choices. The options available enable different audiences to choose information on the topics that interest them, and to follow the news at a level of detail and complexity that suits their level of information literacy. Participation in specific echo chambers and filter bubbles – if such labels apply to these self-selecting information enclaves at all – could therefore even be beneficial, as long as 'people have routes out of the chamber' (O'Hara and Stevens 2015: 417).

More than two decades of research have documented the beneficial aspects of participating in supportive online communities – knowledge that is often absent from popular discussions about the dangers of echo chambers and filter bubbles. Like-minded users can help each other make sense of the world around them, while still often testing one another's perspectives (sometimes aggressively so); there are social *as well as* political aspects even in online communities with an explicitly ideological overtone. To belong to an online community, some degree of agreement and common purpose is required, but this does not mean that participants must adhere to a shared ideology in every aspect of their (online) existence.

Finally, much empirical work on echo chambers and filter bubbles is also shaped by what researchers are able to observe: the active expressions of participating users, in the form of posts, tweets, shares, likes, @mentions, retweets, and their networks of connection and interaction. Even members of a partisan *Facebook* group or followers of an ideologically slanted selection of *Twitter* accounts may have critical or oppositional readings of the content they encounter; their actual ideological stance could only be verified by talking to them. After a decade of substantial enthusiasm about the power of observational, digitally native, 'big data' research methods, this emphasises the continuing importance of media effects and media psychology research – a point to which we will return in chapter 5.

Overall, then, we have considerable reason to temper our enthusiasm for concepts such as 'echo chamber' and 'filter bubble' and to critically interrogate the evidence for and against their existence. In particular, we should be deeply wary of some media and political operatives' ulterior motives for embracing these ideas. For some techno-pessimists, the moral panic has been a useful excuse to maintain a sceptical stance towards all new media: 'see, you Web idealists have been shown up – humankind's social nature sucks, just as we always told you!' (Weinberger 2004: n.p.). Others pursue more specific agendas: concerns over the societal effects of echo chambers and filter bubbles offer an excellent opportunity for struggling commercial news outlets from the pre-digital era to agitate for greater regulation of social media, in a bid to reshape the competition in their own favour.

We must therefore carefully assess claims about the impact of online and social media on political information and societal polarisation. Weinberger warned as early as 2004 that 'this is a myth just waiting to concretize into common wisdom' (2004: n.p.). By now, that concrete has set: 'echo chamber' and 'filter bubble' appear in scholarly and popular discussion, and even in presidential farewell speeches, as if we actually had clear and generally accepted definitions of these terms. Let us now cut through the concrete to reveal the shaky foundations upon which they are built.

TWO

Echo Chambers? Filter Bubbles? What Even Are They?

To determine whether echo chambers and filter bubbles are real, we must first develop a clearer definition of what these terms mean. This is surprisingly difficult: these concepts are rarely explicitly defined and the few definitions we do have vary widely over the years and across the phenomena they seek to describe.

At their core, though, they describe the properties of networks: offline and online; personal, social and professional. They describe how individuals and institutions (news outlets, political parties, activist groups, etc.) in those networks connect with each other, and how they communicate and share information with one another. Echo chambers and filter bubbles come into being when there are significant disconnects in the network: when specific groups and communities separate from the rest of the network (by their own choice or through the actions of others) and can therefore no longer be reached by new information from the outside.

In principle, such occasional disconnects from society are nothing new: they precede social media by several millennia. Echo chambers and filter bubbles are therefore not limited to online environments. However, modern platforms have made enclosures and disconnections more visible, more measurable, and potentially more powerful. Given the increasing role that online and social media play as information conduits and news sources (Newman et al. 2016), we must look especially to echo chambers and filter bubbles in online environments as we try to understand their spread and impact.

Conventional media – including print and broadcast as well as their online extensions – also play an important role here, however: as active participants in the networks themselves or as sources of the information that users circulate through social media. News outlets, influential individuals (politicians, journalists, celebrities, activists) within social networks, and platform providers such as *Google*, *Facebook*, and *Twitter*, serve as 'information intermediaries' (Helberger 2018: 154): in a complex and multifaceted information environment, users rely on them as gatewatchers and news curators (Bruns 2018) to reduce information overload. These intermediaries channel attention and help users find relevant information. Some intermediaries have even assumed quasi-monopolistic roles: this is certainly true for *Google*, whose search engine dominates the market.

Critically, these intermediaries do not limit the ability for diverse ideas and perspectives to be expressed, online or offline: they do not curtail the diversity of information *supply*, but potentially affect the diversity of information that users trusting in such intermediaries are *exposed* to (Helberger 2018: 158). If the information selection mechanisms built into intermediary platforms – directly in the form of search and filtering algorithms, or more indirectly in the user interactions they promote or discourage – privilege the availability and circulation of certain types of information over others, then users' exposure diversity suffers. Ultimately, this assumes that such processes occur in concert across all the channels through which people access information: for example, if a user's online information exposure is limited by the search engine they consult, but they maintain a diverse information diet in their offline news media consumption, then this does not pose a particularly significant concern (cf. Schmidt et al. 2017: 7).

Notwithstanding this broader, multi-platform perspective, much of the early discussion of echo chambers and filter bubbles focused on their potential impacts on single platforms, with definitions changing as the concepts were applied to ever new contexts. Let us now attempt to trace this shape-shifting across several key stages.

Early concerns about our online information diets predate even *Google* itself. In his 1995 book *Being Digital*, Nicholas Negroponte envisaged the *Daily Me*, a highly personalised online newspaper that selects news stories according to the explicit or implicit interests of each user. Still futuristic then, these predictions have been realised at least in part by now, with news websites employing user profiling and algorithmic content selection to such an extent that 'gatekeeping no longer belongs to journalists or humans exclusively' (Nechushtai and Lewis 2019: 299). Although Negroponte did not necessarily present such developments as negative, subsequent commentators highlighted especially the dismantling of a shared knowledge base for all citizens in society that would result from a heavy personalisation and algorithmic curation of news offerings (Zuiderveen Borgesius et al. 2016: 2). For example, President Obama's farewell speech describes the 'splintering of our media into a channel for every taste' (2017: n.p.), threatening democracy itself.

In turn, Negroponte's *Daily Me* is referenced explicitly by the legal scholar Cass Sunstein, the leading proponent of the echo chamber thesis, in his 2001 book *Echo Chambers*. As Sunstein puts it,

> a well-functioning democracy – a republic – depends not just on freedom from censorship,

but also on a set of common experiences and on unsought, unanticipated, and even unwanted exposures to diverse topics, people, and ideas. A system of 'gated communities' is as unhealthy for cyberspace as it is for the real world. (Sunstein 2001a: 2)

Sunstein would go on to further develop this argument across a series of books: *Republic.com* (2001b), *Republic.com 2.0* (2009), and *#Republic* (2017), updating his warnings of the deleterious impact of such echo chambers for an evolving online media environment in which the role of personalised news websites diminished as personalisation in social media spaces increased.

Mid-1990s concerns about information personalisation generally remained at the level of hypothetical thought experiments and extrapolations, largely because news outlets' technological capabilities for user profiling and content personalisation systems were still very poor; the *Daily Me* as foreseen by Negroponte and denounced by Sunstein never eventuated at the time. A more credible threat of informational fragmentation arose with the advent of modern search engines in the late 1990s: now, it did seem possible and even plausible that different users would be offered diverging results by the (undisclosed) search algorithm, customised perhaps based on the user's search history.

19

Eventually emerging from these concerns is our second key concept: the filter bubble. This term was introduced by political activist and tech entrepreneur Eli Pariser, whose 2011 book *The Filter Bubble: What the Internet Is Hiding from You* opens with a reflection on *Google*'s efforts to personalise search results to address a given user's likely interests. Pariser begins with an anecdote:

> in the spring of 2010, while the remains of the Deepwater Horizon oil rig were spewing crude oil into the Gulf of Mexico, I asked two friends to search for the term 'BP'. They're pretty similar – educated white left-leaning women who live in the Northeast. But the results they saw were quite different. One of my friends saw investment information about BP. The other saw news. For one, the first page of results contained links about the oil spill; for the other, there was nothing about it except for a promotional ad from BP. (Pariser 2011: 2)

If such patterns are widespread and systematic, and result from algorithmic selection based on the individual user's interest profile – as opposed to more benign factors, such as breaking news or even built-in randomisation designed to promote source diversity

– they would indeed point to the possibility of filter bubbles. More specifically, these processes might lock users into highly idiosyncratic filter bubbles based purely on their personal interests, or could give rise to collective filter bubbles that enclose groups with broadly similar interests and ideologies in a 'unique information universe' that could facilitate the 'hardening of their own political position' (Krafft et al. 2018: 6; my translation). As Pariser puts it, such algorithms would 'narrow what we know, surrounding us in information that tends to support what we already believe' (Pariser 2015: n.p.).

If such early visions largely explore what is done to users by the personalisation algorithms of news sites or search engines, a more recent stream of discussion focuses more closely on what users do to one another, independently or with the support of platforms and their algorithms. Here, our attention shifts to social media in their early and contemporary forms.

This part of the story begins with the emergence of blogs in the early 2000s: at the time, it was expected that this new publishing format would bring about a shift from the consumption of mainstream news to more active online engagement and discussion, especially of political issues. This raised concerns about a 'cyberbalkanization' of the Internet into networks of blogs with shared ideological views (Adamic and Glance 2005: 37). Here, it is no longer the external force of search and personalisation systems that pushes users into echo chambers or filter bubbles; instead, users actively seek out those sources that best represent their ideological stance, while avoiding those that present the opposing view: a phenomenon known as selective exposure.

The subsequent decline of blogging and the rise of modern social media may have changed the platforms where such processes play out and the vocabulary we use to describe them, but the argument persists: by friending and following selected other accounts, by joining specific *Facebook* pages and groups or participating in particular *Twitter* hashtags, users attach themselves to distinct interest communities while disconnecting from the non-like-minded rest of the social network. Within these interest-based enclaves, a highly selective and self-reinforcing information diet can then circulate unopposed.

From this perspective, echo chambers result from deliberate connection with like-minded others – a tendency known as homophily, which seeks similarity and avoids difference. Psychologically, this is explained by the well-documented affective consequences of exposure to difference: 'people tend to feel stressed and pressured to conform'. This experience makes them seek reinforcement for their original views (Colleoni et al. 2014: 319). In theory, such processes exist well beyond social media, across the entire range of platforms through which an individual consumes information (Zuiderveen Borgesius et al. 2016: 3).

Although, in contrast to the *Daily Me* and personalised search engine recommendations, the processes of social fragmentation envisaged here are thus predominantly driven by user choices, they are also shaped by platform algorithms. Social media platforms routinely filter the activity streams of the various accounts, pages, groups, or hashtags that a given user follows and recommend further accounts and topics that users may be interested in (Helberger 2018: 162). But because this happens continually, rather than in response to explicit personalisation settings or search queries, users of social media platforms are considerably less aware of such algorithmic shaping than when they interact with news recommendation systems or search engines; they assume that 'they see the same content as everybody else' (Zuiderveen Borgesius et al. 2016: 5). From this perspective, social media users could be unaware that they exist in an echo chamber or filter bubble and therefore also lack the motivation to escape from it.

Indeed, much of the current debate about echo chambers and filter bubbles has tended to highlight the agency of algorithmic curation over that of human users (Spohr 2017: 153). This represents a dangerous slide towards a technologically determinist understanding of the contemporary media environment: human agency is sidelined and information diets are inherently and inextricably dictated by the platforms' all-powerful algorithms. In reality, the impacts of algorithms are likely to be considerably less significant, and far from inescapable: users still retain their own agency to make choices about searching, connecting, and engaging with others on a particular issue or topic.

Further, algorithms themselves do not arrive fully formed. The informational preferences built into an algorithm 'are a form of human prejudice that's built into the system' (Koene 2016: n.p.); this prejudice reflects the collective assumptions and understandings of their developers. Platform algorithms may thus variously amplify or counteract the effects of human agency in choosing personalisation options, formulating search terms, or engaging in social networks, but predominantly it is that human agency, rather than some inherent and independent property of the algorithms, that determines whether echo chambers or filter bubbles result from these human choices. We should be deeply wary of arguments based on technological determinism and algorithmic inevitability as we assess these phenomena, therefore.

Indeed, the content promoted or demoted by the platforms' algorithms is itself largely human-made and therefore not without inconsistencies. If we expect, for example, that algorithmic recommendations about whom to follow on a social media platform lead to the creation of ideologically pure echo chambers because they privilege connections between like-minded users and discourage interactions between non-like-minded users, this fundamentally assumes that users are rational and consistent in what they post: that all of their posts will reflect a particular, fixed worldview. But people are considerably more complex than this, using general-purpose social media platforms like *Facebook* and *Twitter* for anything from political debate through entertainment and sports to the maintenance of social ties. What is an algorithm to make of such variable and inconsistent behaviour?

Echo chambers and filter bubbles represent something of a moving target: the places where theorists most expected to encounter them have shifted repeatedly since Negroponte first envisaged his *Daily Me* in 1995, moving from news personalisation through search engines to early and contemporary social media. Along the way, the perceived importance of algorithms in sorting users into echo chambers and filter bubbles has ebbed and flowed as well: though critical to the filter bubble that Pariser saw in search results, in social media they play only one, but not necessarily the most crucial role. Here, they variously amplify or counteract human agency in making homophilous connections that seek similarity and avoid difference.

Given this wide variety of contexts over the past two decades, it is not surprising but nonetheless deeply problematic that we have very few explicit definitions of what these terms actually mean and of how they might be distinguished from one another; indeed, much popular and even scholarly literature tends to use them interchangeably. This definitional vagueness does not help us to determine whether they exist in observable reality at all – and if so, under what circumstances.

Part of the blame for this unfortunate state of affairs belongs squarely with the authors who have popularised these terms. As Weinberger notes in reviewing Cass Sunstein's third iteration of his central work, now called *#Republic* (2017), 'despite his frequent use of the term . . ., Sunstein never defines echo chambers' (Weinberger 2017: n.p.). Eli Pariser does not offer anything more substantial either: he describes the filter bubble as 'a

"We should be deeply
wary of arguments
based on technological
determinism and
algorithmic inevitability."

unique universe of information for each of us' (2011: 9), but otherwise seems to regard his metaphor as self-explanatory. Overall, both Sunstein and Pariser appear less concerned with providing a precise description of what constitutes an echo chamber or filter bubble, or what distinguishes the two concepts, than they are with outlining their substantial negative effects on society and democracy – if indeed they do exist in reality.

Beyond the broad-strokes warnings of Sunstein and Pariser, more scholarly contributions have often similarly taken these concepts to be established, rather than providing an explicit working definition. Where definitions are available, they range from comparatively generic to highly context-specific approaches. To help us cut through this confusion, let us adopt a new and clearer set of definitions that is particularly suited to social media. Further, to avoid and undo the gradual blending of the two concepts into one ill-defined idea, let us make a clearer distinction between echo chambers on the one hand, and filter bubbles on the other. Finally, let us also reject technological determinism by repositioning filter and recommendation algorithms as one, but not the only contributing factor that drives the emergence of echo chambers and filter bubbles and highlight instead the role of human agency in making search, connection, and engagement choices.

With these goals in mind, then, for the remainder of this book let us adopt the following definitions (cf. Bruns 2017):

- An **echo chamber** comes into being when a group of participants choose to preferentially *connect* with each other, to the exclusion of outsiders. The more fully formed this network is (that is, the more connections are created within the group, and the more connections with outsiders are severed), the more isolated from the introduction of outside views is the group, while the views of its members are able to circulate widely within it.

- A **filter bubble** emerges when a group of participants, independent of the underlying network structures of their connections with others, choose to preferentially *communicate* with each other, to the exclusion of outsiders. The more consistently they exercise this choice, the more likely it is that participants' own views and information will circulate amongst group members, rather than any information introduced from the outside.

To understand the distinctions between these two concepts, imagine a network of *Facebook* or *Twitter* accounts that are following only each other, without any links to the wider platform network beyond. By the definition above, these would constitute an echo chamber: as one account in the network posts something, this can reach others in the group, but nobody on the outside. The more densely the members are connected – that is, the more of the others each of them follows – the more quickly and easily does any one of their posts reach everyone else. (The same effect could also be achieved by creating a closed *Facebook* group: here, the platform facilitates a thorough in-group connection and keeps out others.) However, being part of such an echo chamber does not preclude its members from introducing outside information into the community, for example by posting links to content they have encountered elsewhere; in this sense, the echo chamber does not constitute a filter bubble. It also does not mean that users are restricted to communicating only with echo chamber members: on *Twitter*, for instance, they could @mention external accounts even if they do not follow them, and thereby carry the views of echo chamber members beyond the boundaries of its immediate network, or retweet posts from the outside and thus make them visible to the echo chamber.

Conversely, imagine a similar group of accounts that, independent of whom they have chosen to follow or friend, communicate only with each other: they only respond to, comment on, share, @mention, like, and retweet each other's posts, even though they might be networked with a much larger number of other accounts. By the definition above, this would represent a filter bubble: although potentially exposed to a much greater diversity of content through their wider networks, only the information originating from members of this in-group is circulated between them and thereby amplified to greater visibility within the bubble. (On *Twitter*, this could be facilitated by engaging only with the content posted by a particular hashtag community, perhaps.) Being part of such a filter bubble would not preclude them from maintaining peripheral awareness of other perspectives by following a larger and more diverse range of other accounts outside the bubble: defined in this way, the filter bubble is not an echo chamber. But it does mean that its members refrain from visibly engaging with such outside content and instead only communicate with one another.

Focusing on networks of connection and networks of communication, respectively, these definitions highlight different aspects of participation in social media. The effect is further amplified if the membership of an echo chamber overlaps *exactly* with that of a filter bubble, however: in this case, participants only follow *and* only interact with members of the same in-group and are thus entirely cut off from the remainder of the network. While an echo chamber or filter bubble alone already significantly restricts users' exposure to or interaction with a diversity of information, this fully-formed information cocoon would have a far more comprehensive impact on the information diet encountered. We can therefore now test for three aspects of a given user's social media experience: are they part of an echo chamber; are they part of a filter bubble; and do those two networks overlap?

Importantly, these definitions do not predetermine the role of algorithms: how participants choose to preferentially connect or communicate with each other is likely to result from a mixture of personal choice and algorithmic curation that is different in each case. As networks form, users may receive recommendations for whom else to follow, or see posts from particular contacts highlighted; as they act on such recommendations, these algorithmic interventions may serve to intensify the interconnections between echo chamber or filter bubble participants and deepen their disconnect from the rest of the network. This feedback loop between human and algorithm may be more or less efficient, depending on the implementation of recommender and filtering algorithms on specific platforms.

A critical observer might ask whether, in light of the fuzziness of these concepts to date, it is sensible to continue with them at all: why introduce better definitions and not just abandon them altogether? Although tempting, the problem is that 'echo chamber' and 'filter bubble' – like the similarly problematic 'fake news' – will continue to be used and misused by journalists, politicians, and the general public even if scholars abandon them; as researchers, our best opportunity to exert meaningful influence is instead to promote more precise definitions that distinguish the two concepts clearly, and to use these definitions to rigorously evaluate the claims made by Sunstein, Pariser, and other proponents of echo chambers and filter bubbles.

Importantly, one key additional benefit of the redefinition introduced here is that it moves these concepts away from simple binary assessments (users either are caught in an echo chamber or filter bubble, or they are not) and towards the measurement of a user's degree of 'chamberness' or 'bubbleness' – that is, of their communicative enclosure. For any given population of users, we can observe and quantify the extent to which they connect or communicate only within the group or also engage with others in the network beyond. This raises other questions that much past research has overlooked: when does mild preferential attachment to like-minded others become dysfunctional avoidance of alternative perspectives? What level of interconnection with the world beyond one's immediate neighbourhood is necessary to maintain a 'healthy' information diet while preventing information overload?

Such questions connect our discussion to a much older tradition of sociological inquiry into the trajectories of information and opinion across society – a tradition that stretches back at least as far as the famous studies of information flows and opinion leadership in suburban and professional networks by Paul Lazarsfeld and Elihu Katz in the 1940s and 1950s (e.g. Katz and Lazarsfeld 1955). That individuals cluster into groups in which communication is faster, more effective, and centred around shared interests and ideologies is nothing new, as we know from such studies: the more critical concern is at what point in-groups that offer support to their members morph into exclusive cliques that actively shun outsiders.

Finally, the redefinition of echo chambers and filter bubbles introduced here takes an explicitly agnostic approach to the nature and content of the information exchanged between participants: these communicative formations might exist amongst communities of music fans just as much as between groups of political extremists. Therefore, even if we can prove their existence in the wild, we should still not assume that echo chambers or filter bubbles necessarily have a negative impact on society and democracy: they become 'problematic only for politically incendiary topics and for highly diverging perspectives' (Krafft et al. 2018: 7; my translation). Indeed, even political information cocoons only pose a problem if the individuals caught in them on one platform are also caught in similar exclusionary environments across all the other information platforms they use (or only draw on a single platform for their information): if they received highly ideologically skewed information from their *Facebook* network, but accessed more balanced news sources through their news apps or offline channels, then their overall exposure to news and information is still characterised by considerable diversity. In such cases, even echo chambers and filter bubbles might not necessarily exert any meaningful effects on those who frequent them.

Overall, the new and more explicit definitions that we have introduced in this chapter make it possible to review and assess with more clarity the evidence both for and against echo chambers and filter bubbles that recent scholarship has compiled. We do so in chapters 3 and 4.

THREE

Echo Chambers and Filter Bubbles in Action

Over the years, a number of studies have claimed to present evidence for echo chambers and filter bubbles. It remains to be seen, however, whether these analyses withstand critical scrutiny especially against a more stringent, systematic definition for these terms; some such apparent echo chambers or filter bubbles may be little more than densely networked communities of interest, or highly partisan and polarised groups within a shared communicative environment.

One of the most influential, comparatively early studies was an analysis by Adamic and Glance (2005) of the patterns of interlinkages amongst political bloggers ahead of the 2004 US presidential election. Assessing network patterns both for connections through blog-rolls (static lists of links to fellow bloggers, presented in a sidebar on the blog) and for links embedded in individual blog posts (a form of communication at a distance between bloggers), the researchers observed a considerable division between liberal and conservative blogs, with substantial hyperlink connections amongst

"Over the years, a number of studies have claimed to present evidence for echo chambers and filter bubbles."

the partisan blogs on either side, but substantially fewer interconnections – only 15% of all links – across ideological camps (Adamic and Glance 2005: 40).

Using the definitions introduced in the previous chapter, we might consider the blogroll patterns as evidence of an echo chamber, and the blog post network as pointing to filter bubbles. Indeed, extrapolating beyond their own data, the researchers compared such preferential, partisan interlinkages to similar partisan patterns in offline media, especially conservative talk radio (Adamic and Glance 2005: 40). It is also clear that such potential echo chambers or filter bubbles – online and offline – are at best imperfectly formed, because a smaller but significant undercurrent of cross-ideological interlinkage remains: Adamic and Glance themselves only regard the progressive and conservative blog networks 'as mild echo chambers' (2005: 41). The two communities are certainly divided – but they are not entirely disconnected.

As long as it remains 'mild', such division ahead of a hard-fought national election (the first since 9/11 and the US invasions of Afghanistan and Iraq) is neither unexpected nor particularly troubling; it fails to support the more dramatic visions of a highly fragmented populace that the echo chamber and filter bubble theses conjure up. In particular, even despite their ideological divisions, the two partisan groups remained united by the mainstream media sources they referenced: although each side also showed strong interest in overtly partisan media outlets (*Fox News* and *National Review* on the right, *Salon* on the left), both linked to the *New York Times* and *Washington Post* with similar frequency (Adamic and Glance 2005: 42). The two partisan communities existed not only within a single shared blogosphere, but also within a common overarching mediasphere – there were no separate information cocoons.

This very limited separation of each partisan community does not warrant a description as echo chamber or filter bubble in the full sense, therefore. On each side, there clearly is some preferential attachment and engagement based on shared ideologies, but the disconnect between them – and from the wider mainstream media – is *too* mild to create any deleterious effects. This is perhaps unsurprising, given the early timeframe of this study. But in contrast to the decentralised and disorganised blogosphere of the early 2000s, the mature social media of today – such as *Twitter* and *Facebook* – operate through central platforms that make it far easier for participants to connect and communicate with like-minded others. Do their advanced social affordances, together with the algorithmic assistance they provide for finding fellow travellers, amplify divisions in the network from 'mild' to more severe?

For *Twitter*, several recent studies suggest that this is the case. Such studies often centre on partisan hashtag communities: Williams et al. (2015), for example, examined the communication patterns of users engaged in discussions about anthropogenic climate change. They found that activity in climate-related hashtags was driven by a small number of highly engaged power users, with more casual participants showing considerably less long-term commitment (Williams et al. 2015: 128). The study grouped leading participants according to their attitudes towards climate change (accepting or denying the scientific consensus; users with neutral or indistinct stance were excluded from the analysis). The balance between these groups varies by hashtag: the cynically-named #climaterealists attracts considerably more denialists than the generic #climatechange.

However, any user can post to any existing *Twitter* hashtag or introduce a new hashtag simply by pre-pending '#' to a keyword. Hashtags themselves are therefore unsuitable as vehicles for echo chambers or filter bubbles: they are simply too porous and too open to new participants and new content to sustain the disconnect that echo chambers and filter bubbles require.

At best, the persistent core of participants in a hashtag community again represents a 'mild' echo chamber, with similarly limited effects on users' information diets.

Usefully, Williams et al. advance beyond hashtags themselves by also examining the follower networks amongst those most active participants, and exploring the patterns of retweets and @mentions between them. The analysis of follower networks is especially valuable because it examines networking patterns beyond the hashtags themselves: arguably, such follower networks influence the day-to-day information consumption of *Twitter* users far more than hashtags. For highly active participants, and for user communities participating in hashtags with scientific or denialist emphasis, the study found strong evidence of homophily: climate change activists predominantly followed other activists, denialists predominantly followed other denialists, and follower relationships across these boundaries were rare. For Williams et al., this meant that 98% of these highly active users were 'members of an echo chamber' (2015: 131).

Notably, however, for retweets and @mentions between these accounts the patterns diverged substantially. Much like follower relationships, retweets were strongly homophilous: activists and denialists each retweeted mainly within their own communities – using the definitions introduced in the previous chapter, this would point to a filter bubble, if retweeting indicates agreement with the views expressed in a message. @mentions, however, also occurred between opposing camps and demonstrate the continuing contestation and acrimony between both sides. Williams et al. conclude that 94% of all users were members of what (by our definition) would be retweet-based filter bubbles, but only 68% were also members of @mention-based filter bubbles (2015: 131).

This appears to provide some solid evidence for echo chambers and filter bubbles on *Twitter*. It also underlines the importance of the more precise and distinct definitions we introduced in the previous chapter: the frequent participants Williams et al. focused on may exist in networks of follower *connections* that exclude opposing views – in echo chambers – but their *communication* patterns through @mentions show that this does not necessarily create similarly exclusive filter bubbles. They may follow only their own, but still argue with the world beyond.

More careful consideration complicates this picture, however. First, much of the investigation is limited to the small community of most active participants within each hashtag. But the less engaged group of casual participants contributes to the hashtags, too; it interacts with core users and each other through retweets and @mentions; it may follow and be followed by the most active users. In this sense, the most committed core constitutes only the tip of the iceberg of a much larger network of connections and communication. It is likely that less engaged participants further from the core of the discussion will also make less ideologically pure decisions about whom to follow, retweet, and @mention; their contributions to the debate therefore facilitate a more inclusive and intermeshed flow of information across entrenched positions. This connective, bridging role across ideological camps is also played by the users with an indistinct stance towards climate science that the study excluded from its analysis.

The conclusion that the study shows 'strong attitude-based homophily and widespread segregation of users into like-minded communities' (Williams et al. 2015: 135) seems premature, therefore. Indeed, the researchers do note that 'we also identified mixed-attitude communities in which users were frequently exposed to a diversity of viewpoints' (2015: 135), and attitudes will be increasingly mixed and muddled away from the central, attitudinally orthodox core of any given network. At this greater distance, participants may also rely less on hashtags as a central source of information, and more on their follower networks:

less engaged users are unlikely to follow thematic hashtags like #climatechange or #climaterealists with great attention, day to day. We must therefore look beyond inherently ideologically defined hashtags, and indeed beyond hashtags themselves, as a mechanism for shaping connections and communication flows.

Garimella et al. (2018) advance in these directions. They identify users participating in political *and* non-political hashtags, focusing (in politics) especially on two-sided rather than multi-sided controversies. Rather than merely inferring users' political leanings from their tweets, this study draws on the URLs shared in tweets to establish participants' ideological preferences. This, of course, requires a placement of news sources along a left-to-right scale. Further, Garimella et al. also capture the networks of accounts followed by each user, to pinpoint which tweets (and embedded URLs) from other hashtag participants a given user is most likely to have encountered.

Somewhat unsurprisingly, the results show that the difference between political and non-political hashtags 'is stark' (Garimella et al. 2018: 917). Users of political hashtags who predominantly post links to partisan news outlets are also more likely to receive links to news sites with similar orientation in the tweets from the other hashtag participants they follow; for non-political hashtags this is not the case. The researchers conclude that 'echo chambers are prevalent on Twitter' (Garimella et al. 2018: 913); using our new definitions, however, it would be more accurate to suggest that the echo chambers represented by the follower networks amongst like-minded users shape the flow of news between them in such a way that filter bubbles also become more likely.

How inescapable is this conclusion, though? Garimella et al. acknowledge that they 'focused on politically-savvy users on Twitter' and that echo chambers may not be 'as pronounced for the general public' (2018: 921). There are further concerns: first, users examined here were identified by selecting – for the political datasets – highly divisive, US-centric topics such as #obamacare, #guncontrol, and #abortion. Second, the study examines only those tweets that users posted into these hashtags; it does not explore what other, possibly less partisan and polarised content they posted in other topical or everyday discussions on *Twitter*. Third, inferring a user's political leaning from the news URLs shared in those tweets necessarily ignores potentially critical, oppositional sharing: in sharing a link to a partisan story, for instance, the user might also critique the content of the article; in this case, the source's leaning is diametrically opposed to the user's. Fourth, any assessment of the political leaning of news sources is far from unproblematic: not every article even in a partisan outlet is necessarily political, or equally biased towards the same side; for example, a generally pro-gun control outlet might run an op-ed by a gun control critic to facilitate debate.

Finally, and most crucially, the analysis is limited to URL tweets exchanged across the follower networks of participants in these hashtags. We have no information about the follower networks of these accounts beyond their fellow hashtag contributors, or about the tweets (and URLs) exchanged across those networks. Somebody who posts highly partisan content into a hashtag on an already intensely polarised issue may well choose their broader connections according to ideological alignment, and the URLs introduced into this broader network may also share that common partisan leaning, but the present study does not provide the evidence to make this logical leap.

Indeed, before we use this evidence of substantial news sourcing polarisation in highly polarised hashtags to jump to conclusions about the overall prevalence of echo chambers or filter bubbles on *Twitter*, consider that the same study also shows a pronounced *absence* of polarisation for apolitical, non-partisan hashtags such as #love, #gameofthrones, or #foodporn. If the partisans populating the political hashtags are so narrow in their utilisation of *Twitter* that they would never stoop to participating in such non-political hashtags, and to connecting and communicating with the non-partisan users found there and in the wider Twittersphere, then their follower networks may indeed constitute a distinct echo chamber, and their interactions with each other might represent a true filter bubble. However, this is unlikely to be a binary, in/out question; rather, their enclosure in echo chambers and filter bubbles should be measured by the *degree* of their disconnection from other, alternative perspectives. The highly partisan groups identified by Garimella et al. (2018) for highly polarised hashtags may advance beyond 'mild' and towards more severe enclosure – but these hashtags and the topics they address constitute only a small subset of the full range of topics and uses observed on *Twitter*, and such echo chambers and filter bubbles therefore still constitute an exception rather than a common pattern on this platform. Importantly, other studies have demonstrated that hashtags and similar connective affordances are 'flexible and situation-specific' and their polarisation 'depends heavily on the nature of the issue' they address (Barberá *et al.* 2015: 1539).

On *Facebook*, most user activity is private and therefore impossible to analyse for outside researchers.

Investigations here have therefore focused on its public spaces: they usually study *Facebook* pages where page operators and users interact without a need for all participants to reciprocally friend one another. Like the *Twitter* research we have discussed, such studies typically select pages dealing with inherently partisan and polarised debates. Bessi (2016) and Quattrociocchi et al. (2016), for example, both contrast activity in scientific and conspiracy theory pages and find that these pages serve as rallying points for very different communities of users: participants will engage with one type of page, but not the other.

Smith and Graham (2017) present a detailed study of one particular community of science denialists: antivaccination activists. Similar to observations on *Twitter*, they find that these are dominated by a small core of highly active participants, active across multiple such pages; less active participants are merely '"transient" visitors' to these pages (2017: 9). This could imply that *Facebook* pages support the formation of tightly connected echo chambers at least amongst core contributors; although impossible for outside researchers, further investigation of the personal networks between contributors' profiles (the *Facebook* equivalent of studying *Twitter*'s follower networks) could lend support to this hypothesis. If they gather on *Facebook* pages *and* show close connections between their profiles while excluding others who are not part of the same in-group, this would indeed constitute a significant echo chamber.

However, Smith and Graham also warn that these networks 'are relatively sparse or "loose"' and 'do not necessarily function as close-knit communities' (2017: 14). Any echo chamber at the core of these communities, therefore, does not extend to more occasional visitors. Even casual exposure, however, could still 'reinforce and cement anti-vaccination beliefs' (2017: 14) and facilitate the rapid and widespread transmission of ideas from the core group to a much larger audience. Smith and Graham describe this as a potential 'filter bubble effect that reinforces anti-vaccination sentiment and practice' (2017: 14), but the mechanisms of this filter bubble remain unclear. The core-and-periphery structure could aid the amplification of anti-vaccination messages through distribution via casual participants (potentially also to their personal, profile-level networks on the platform). But this is not an exclusionary filter bubble designed to intensify issue identification and orthodoxy amongst a self-selecting in-group as defined in the previous chapter; it represents a considerably more outwardly focused, quasi-messianic initiative to convince others of the anti-scientific, anti-vaccination message. If this is a bubble, its aim is not to be impervious to counter-attitudinal views from the outside, but to enlarge the bubble to include as many converts as possible. A communicative disconnect from the rest of the world, as our definition requires it, would be counterproductive.

Importantly, Smith and Graham consider in some detail the role of *Facebook*'s affordances and algorithms in supporting such processes. If *Facebook* encourages small, densely connected networks, they suggest, this crucially enables like-minded groups 'to blossom, flourish, and resist being dismantled or disrupted by outside influences' (2017: 14). *Facebook*'s recommendation and newsfeed algorithms draw on the user's past activities on and beyond the platform to highlight other contributors and content they may be interested in engaging with. As *Facebook* users visit anti-vaccination pages, is *Facebook* likely to recommend further anti-vaccination content and activists, and will this complement or replace mainstream, scientifically sound perspectives on the topic? Might it also suggest counterfactual theories other than anti-vaccination activism itself, and thereby draw users deeper and deeper into an alternate universe of conspiracy theorists and disinformation peddlers?

Smith and Graham remain cautious on this point (2017: 14). Such caution is justified: given the proprietary, blackboxed nature of *Facebook*'s algorithms and the frequent adjustments it makes to how they function, their exact operation remains unknown (and indeed unknowable for independent, critical, outside research-ers). At best, their fundamental operating assumptions could be inferred from a careful, long-term, forensic analysis of the results they produce, for a wide range of users with diverse identities and topical interests.

What are we to make of these necessarily brief but nonetheless representative snapshots of claims to echo chambers and filter bubbles in contemporary social media platforms, based on empirical research at a variety of scales? We have encountered tendencies for ideologically orthodox groups of core participants to form within groups of users addressing topics of shared concern, especially when those topics are political and polarising; such patterns appear less pronounced or even absent for topics that are apolitical or fail to divide participants along faultlines of 'progressive' and 'con-servative', 'left' and 'right', 'for' and 'against'.

The formation of such partisan groups is a function of homophily: the preferential attachment to like-minded others. 'This promotes extremism' (O'Hara 2014: 79), or at least a growing partisanship that could foment extremist views. If users really do form strongly homophilous networks, to the exclusion of others, then it is also possible that they increasingly communicate only with these fellow travellers; the echo chamber of *connections* would thus be augmented by a filter bubble of *communication*, and increasing overlap between the two might hermetically disconnect this self-reinforcing network of partisans from the outside world with its challenging, critical views.

As this cocoon forms, peer-group pressure will also discourage internal dissent, following the logic of the 'spiral of silence' (Noelle-Neumann 1974): the more acutely members of the community perceive the attitudes of those around them, the more they also 'adopt positions which look good to their peers' (O'Hara 2014: 79) and avoid challenging the perceived communal consensus – which would undermine the member's own standing within that community. Indeed, to the extent that the community rewards adherence to a shared orthodoxy with increased social status within the group, the spiral of silence may even feed a spiral of ideological reinforcement, as participants outdo each other in displaying their commitment to the community's shared beliefs (O'Hara 2014: 80–1; cf. Yardi and boyd 2010: 318). Platform algorithms that detect such patterns might further amplify them, by preferentially displaying the posts from the most central, ideologically orthodox community members and thereby further cementing their status as an example to emulate; this would be an algorithmic spiral of silence and reinforcement.

Such homophily is especially powerful when the community's central beliefs can be expressed in the simplest possible terms. It will surprise no-one that a recent study found the core participants in the Trump campaign hashtag #MAGA ('Make America Great Again') to be 'nationalists or ultraconservatives', and strongly antagonistic towards liberal views (Chong 2018: 460). But most debates are not so simply reducible to a matter of 'for' and 'against' and do not engender such fervent partisanship amongst their contestants. In those cases, a clearly defined in-group of like-minded participants will be considerably more difficult to find, spirals of silence or reinforcement will take much longer to get started, and algorithms may highlight users and posts representative of *multiple* sides of the argument – not just of one of them.

Large-scale studies of social media discussion patterns – again focusing mainly only on hashtag and keyword use on *Twitter*, unfortunately – support such observations. 'Polarized crowds' are typical for controversies between 'liberal' and 'conservative' groups, at least in a US context (Smith et al. 2014: 1). Yet because they share the same hashtags (Smith et al. 2014: 20), they are far from invisible to each other; participants who follow the hashtag or search for keywords relevant to the debate would readily encounter a range of views. Paradoxically, the more publicly visible partisan communities make themselves – for instance by adopting prominent hashtags on *Twitter* – the more they also expose themselves to access and interaction by their opponents; the cross-ideological @mentioning in the hashtags studied by Williams et al. (2015) demonstrates this. Deliberate cross-cutting also occurs frequently between opposing partisan hashtags, in fact: as early as 2010, Yardi and boyd noted that, during political discussions about abortion rights on *Twitter*, users included 'pairs of hashtags in their tweets' to address both their own side and take the argument to their opponents. This way, the tweet authors made sure that followers of these hashtags saw both sides of the debate (2010: 317).

Indeed, the echo chambers and filter bubbles we have encountered so far were not hermetically sealed off from their surrounding communicative environments (Zuiderveen Borgesius et al. 2016: 9): their extent of 'chamberness' and 'bubbleness' is a measurable feature of each network's permeability to outside connection and communication. The more 'mild' such tendencies are, however, the more indistinguishable they are from ordinary communities of interest, online and offline: if the homophilous connection with like-minded others creates no more than an increased support network, but does not insulate users from exposure to difference, do such incomplete and nonexclusive information cocoons matter at all? Notably, Beam and Kosicki even suggest that this more benign form of homophily 'may facilitate increased exposure to news' (2014: 61): users within like-minded communities benefit from the material shared by their connections.

But our understanding of the vast social media spaces of *Twitter* and *Facebook* (not to mention other, considerably less researched platforms) remains thoroughly limited by the methodological approaches employed in their study. A focus on hashtags and public pages, at best augmented by further exploration of follower networks or larger-scale comparative analysis across multiple divergent cases, still dominates. The selection of such examples from all possible cases necessarily and directly influences the outcomes of the research. In other words, what we find on mass-population social media platforms depends crucially on where we look: partisan pages and hashtags will appear to support echo chambers and filter bubbles, while spaces of cross-partisan engagement will show evidence of genuine debate (cf. Wojcieszak and Mutz 2009: 42).

If there is some limited evidence of echo chambers and filter bubbles in contexts of considerable partisanship, then, how typical and representative are such communities for ordinary social media users and their everyday practices? If the Twittersphere consists 'of a multitude of small clusters that function largely independently and in a decentralised fashion' (Yang et al. 2017: 1997), we must observe a large number of such independent clusters (centred around shared identity or interests) to establish whether similar group dynamics are at play in each of them, or whether they have evolved distinct patterns; the same is true for the considerably more complex networks of *Facebook* and other platforms. Such research is rendered difficult if not impossible also by the fact that much user activity takes place in private or semi-private spaces that nonetheless feed into more public communicative processes; for obvious ethical and practical reasons, such private activity is unobservable for researchers working without the support of the platforms.

On *Twitter*, much political discussion takes place outside of the hashtags that nominally provide a space for such debate, precisely because users are reluctant to expose their views to the greater, unknown audience of the hashtag; avoiding hashtags means that tweets will reach only the user's followers and therefore a somewhat more knowable audience. On *Facebook*, the same calculus means that most users will keep their political opinions to their personal profiles rather than engaging with explicitly political, public pages. For example, even during an election campaign, only 11.2% of Polish users engaged with explicitly political *Facebook* pages (Batorski and Grzywińska 2018: 368): evidently, users preferred the more private environs of their friendship networks.

This focus on engaging within personal networks also indicates a preference for the comparative diversity of genuinely social networks over the polarisation and orthodoxy of explicitly political pages, groups, hashtags and other public spaces. This highlights one of the key flaws of the filter bubble concept. Eli Pariser suggests that

> using Facebook means you'll tend to see significantly more news that's popular among people who share your political beliefs. . . . The Facebook news feed algorithm in particular will tend to amplify news that your political compadres favor. (Pariser 2015: n.p.)

But the fundamental fallacy implied in this view is that people use *Facebook* (and other platforms) in the first place to talk about politics, or that they make their friend and follower connections primarily because of shared political ideology. Surveys of US social media users ahead of the 2016 presidential election suggest that such partisan selectivity is a minority approach: only '23% of Facebook users and 17% of Twitter users say [that] most of the people in their networks hold political beliefs similar to theirs' (Duggan and Smith 2016: 9). This means that the remainder – more than three-quarters of *Facebook* users and more than two-fifths of *Twitter* users – are exposed to a variety of political perspectives, if indeed their connections talk about politics at all.

The picture becomes even more complicated once we recognise that all the studies we have encountered so far have focus on single platforms. But users engage with a diverse ecosystem of online platforms (Vaccari et al. 2016: 10) – so what does it mean to be locked into an echo chamber of like-minded connections, or to experience an ideologically pure feed of communication within a filter bubble, on *Twitter* or *Facebook* alone, if one's *other* social and informational networks are not so one-sided? Even a hyperpartisan, single-minded hashtag warrior on *Twitter* might still be embedded in an attitudinally diverse family and friendship network on *Facebook* and therefore encounter a wide range of perspectives from outside the bubble (Dubois and Blank 2018a: 735) – to say nothing of their further connections offline.

We should not jump to generalisations from the limited number of suspected echo chambers and filter bubbles identified on specific platforms in particular circumstances, therefore – either to claim the uncontested applicability of these results across the entire platform or even across all social media in spite of their considerable social and organisational differences, or to suggest that the users enclosed in such cocoons on *one* platform are also cut off from healthier information and communication diets in all *other* aspects of their social and intellectual lives. We must also recognise temporal and geographic specificities: many studies focus on extraordinary circumstances (election campaigns or acute political crises) or examine only one local or national political context. In particular, the peculiarities of US politics render it a 'deviant' rather than typical case by international comparison (Valeriani and Vaccari 2016: 1862). This was already true before the election of Donald Trump and even more so amidst the permanent hyperpoliticised crisis since. While clearly this American malaise now also threatens to infect other democracies, many have not yet experienced social and societal disintegration to a similar degree as the United States – not least because of their considerably different media and political systems.

Finally, if echo chambers and filter bubbles seem most likely in highly hyperpartisan, ideologically ortho-dox communities, let us also consider the possible motivations for cross-cutting information exposure that exist in such communities. It is certainly possible that partisans retreat into such spaces, connecting only with their 'political compadres', to avoid 'inadvertent expo-sure' to views they disagree with (Brundidge 2010: 687). However, it is especially these most partisan ideologues who need to track 'counter-attitudinal information' (Garrett et al. 2013: 118): to most effectively defend and promote their own ideological identity, even only within the partisan community itself, they must know how the other side thinks and what counter-arguments it might offer (Weeks et al. 2016: 251). From this per-spective, 'engaging with the enemy does not necessarily make a group less partisan' (O'Hara and Stevens 2015: 418): it strengthens in-group identification by provid-ing an outside 'other' that serves as an embodiment of the political enemy.

A considerable range of studies supports this per-spective. In general, well beyond social media, highly partisan political supporters are also intense users of mainstream media sources (Garrett 2009b: 688); on *Twitter*, 'conspiracy theorists tweet articles from sites that deny the conspiracy theories, but do so in a confrontational way – often as more evidence of their theory' (Starbird 2017b: 7). In other words, such users deliberately burst their ideological filter bubbles to present an oppositional reading of the outside content this enables them to encounter. The same is true for echo chambers: here, too, those with tendencies 'toward uncivil behavior on social media' often extend their networks across ideological divides explicitly in order to attack, insult, upset, and troll their opponents (Groshek and Koc-Michalska 2017: 1401). Such practices are disruptive and dysfunctional, and driven by highly populist and partisan attitudes – but echo chambers and filter bubbles they are not.

Overall, then, *especially* the most hyperpartisan ideologues can least afford to disappear into echo chambers and filter bubbles; to attract others to their cause, to monitor what oppositional voices are saying, and to express counter-arguments for the faithful, they must remain connected. Consequentially, several studies have shown that the use of partisan news sites goes hand in hand with the consumption of mainstream news (Garrett et al. 2013: 122). This represents a fundamental paradox in populist communication: 'populists denounce the "lying press"' yet still rely on it for material (Krämer 2017: 1303).

In spite of the mild or not-so-mild, issue- and platform-specific echo chambers and filter bubbles that various studies appear to have found, then, this broader consideration of the practices and motivations of ordinary users and hyperpartisan activists makes us question the real effects of such phenomena and the role of online and social media in driving them. We have always made choices about whom we connect with and what information we consume (Zuiderveen Borgesius et al. 2016: 10). Even if these selection and exclusion processes now take place through new media platforms, what if anything is new about them, and why would the use of online technologies make any significant difference (Brundidge 2010: 682)?

To be sure, digital media technologies have improved our ability to connect and communicate across distance, aiding the growth and integration of what previously were obscure, dispersed groupings, including ideological movements. This, however, is a question less about connection or disconnection as a result of echo chambers and filter bubbles and much more about the role of online and social media in the efficient organisation of fringe, hyperpartisan, and possibly explicitly antidemocratic elements. But while it is important to fight such extremists and the causes they support, they nonetheless constitute only a small minority of users and should not colour our overall perception of online and social media. The media diets of most ordinary citizens remain balanced and moderate, and the hyper-partisans are in the minority even within their overall ideological camps (Guess 2016: 18). The same is true for political debate: even in the dysfunctional context of the 2016 US election, only some political partisans enjoyed the ideological fight, while most others felt 'annoyance and aggravation' at the tone and content of political discussions on their social media platforms (Duggan and Smith 2016: 3).

There is therefore a danger that we are paying far too much attention to the aberrant practices of a handful of 'political junkies' (Coleman 2003) rather than the experiences of ordinary, mostly politically disinterested citizens. The latter are neither likely to be caught in echo chambers nor to be trapped in filter bubbles; their activities exhibit preferential attachment to one connection over another, but such preferences are determined by a combination of factors, not simply by ideology. Indeed, the fact that they make such selections for a wide spectrum of reasons, across a range of online and offline platforms, also means that the network and communicative enclosure that 'hard' echo chambers and filter bubbles would imply is especially unlikely: 'even if one network has an unhealthy effect . . ., it doesn't follow that it's the only influence on those within it' (O'Hara 2014: 80).

Such more multifaceted approaches to online and social media, and the connective and communicative outcomes that result from them, are documented by a range of studies that move beyond the observation of select hashtags, pages, and other highly specific communicative spaces in social media and beyond. Chapter 4 presents this research, exploring its implications for the idea of echo chambers and filter bubbles.

FOUR

Bursting the Bubble

The studies we encountered in the previous chapter lent only very qualified support to Sunstein's and Pariser's thesis of the damaging effects of echo chambers and filter bubbles on society and democracy. Others have gone considerably further in challenging these concepts. They have examined user activity patterns on social media platforms such as *Facebook* and *Twitter* and returned to the much older question of filter bubbles in search results.

For *Facebook*, major studies by Beam et al. used survey data from US-based respondents during the 2014 mid-term congressional election (2018a) and 2016 presidential election (2018b) to explore the impact of social media on news engagement and political polarisation. In stark contrast to fears about increasing homophily and isolation along ideological divides, they found 'that social media use can lead to pro-social outcomes': users with diverse social networks engage with a greater variety of news (Beam et al. 2018a: 2309). As a general-purpose social network,

Facebook enables and actively encourages users to connect with others, including contacts as disparate as family, friends, co-workers, casual acquaintances, communities of interest, and even (mainly via public pages) celebrities, sportspeople, and politicians. Users who embed themselves in such heterogeneous, multifaceted networks frequently experience 'context collapse' (Marwick & boyd 2011): their connections like, share, and comment on the same posts, and interact with one another despite the widely diverging social contexts in which they know the individual at the centre of this personal network. *Facebook* profiles are a crucial engine of context collapse.

Facebook does offer mechanisms for segregating such different social contacts: making specific posts visible only to immediate friends, or defining distinct collections of contacts to whom posts can then be directed. But such features for controlling information flows are too complex and tedious to be widely used: most users direct posts at any and all of their connections (Beam et al. 2018a: 2298; Sleeper et al. 2013). Platform algorithms, too, could avoid context collapse by selectively highlighting the posts from only one of the social groups with whom a given user is connected; however, faced with an inherently diverse range of contacts, all of whom the user has chosen to connect with, how would they make such a choice? *Facebook* users have gradually resigned themselves to the inevitability of context collapse, or even recognise it as a built-in benefit: context collapse exposes them to a wider range of content and views than they would encounter within a homogeneous in-group of close relations (cf. Vriens and van Ingen 2018: 2436).

This more varied information diet offers diverse political perspectives; it also generates more news engagement, 'both through more sharing and reading news online' (Beam *et al.* 2018a: 2305). The pattern holds even in the highly combative and polarised environment of the 2016 US presidential election: here, engagement with news via *Facebook* even appeared to drive 'a modest over-time spiral of depolarization' (Beam *et al.* 2018b: 940). Rather than settling ever more tightly into echo chambers of like-minded partisans or filter bubbles of attitude-reinforcing propaganda, users with partisan perspectives were exposed, willingly or not, to contrary perspectives, and such serendipitous encounters encouraged them to moderate their more fervently held beliefs. These findings, Beam et al. conclude, 'debunk the theoretical links between social and algorithmic recommendations of news on social media and filter bubbles and echo chambers' (2018b: 951); in fact, they suggest that context collapse in *Facebook* users' social networks actively militates against their enclosure in information cocoons.

While these studies examine *Facebook* at the level of personal profiles, others have investigated how *Facebook* users engage with public pages. Pages enable otherwise unconnected users to engage with each other and with page operators; they show broader, public structures of interest and attention. A study for leading German newspaper *Süddeutsche Zeitung* ahead of the country's 2017 federal election explored patterns of engagement with popular *Facebook* pages by users who also like one or more of the major parties' *Facebook* pages, offering a novel perspective on divisions in the interest and information diets of users in different political camps (Brunner and Ebitsch 2017; Rietzschel 2017). 'Apparently closed filter bubbles do not exist in large parts of the political spectrum in Germany' (Rietzschel 2017: n.p.; my translation): from the socialist Left Party to the conservative Christian Democrats, interests overlap and information travels freely. Users follow a set of leading information, entertainment, and sports pages that hardly varies despite the different political convictions that their interest in specific party pages indicates. In particular, they follow the same leading news sources (Brunner and Ebitsch 2017).

A major exception from this generally unfragmented media and information diet are followers of the far-right extremist Alternative für Deutschland (AfD) party, however. Sixty-two of the 100 most popular *Facebook* pages liked by users who follow the AfD's page are not found in the top hundred pages liked by followers of other parties. This demonstrates both the considerable unity in interests amongst AfD partisans and their significant divergence from the German political mainstream. This holds for general-interest content as well as news pages: AfD supporters do not follow the pages of mainstream news outlets, but read hyperpartisan content instead (Brunner and Ebitsch 2017). Similarly, the followers of established, democratic parties also like entertainment, comedy, and football pages; the AfD followers' focus remains on migration politics and shows little evidence of a more rounded set of interests (Brunner and Ebitsch 2017).

These significant distinctions suggest that, if echo chambers and filter bubbles exist amongst German *Facebook* users at all, they do so only in extremist contexts. 'Contrary to the filter bubble thesis, many citizens apparently still share something like a collective public sphere, even on Facebook' (Rietzschel 2017: n.p.; my translation), where connections and communication bridge party divides. This makes sense in the German multi-party system, where parties even from considerably diverging ideological backgrounds often work together to form stable coalition governments. Only the AfD and its supporters, who reject this consensus-based democratic model in favour of an autocratic and polarising style of politics, inhabit a separate echo chamber of connections around shared populist obsessions, which may also give rise to a filter bubble of exclusionary in-group communication. This poses a critical challenge to society and democracy, in Germany and wherever else populists have emerged as disruptive forces, but does not support the general thesis that online and social media inevitably fragment society and enclose individuals and groups in information cocoons. Whether *Facebook* and other platforms materially aid the rise of the AfD and similar extremist parties, or enable the political mainstream to sustain a cross-ideological public sphere, depends on who uses them.

Studies of connection and interaction patterns on *Twitter* also support this perspective. Vaccari et al. (2016) surveyed Italian and German users who had used politically relevant keywords and hashtags during the two countries' 2013 elections, and found indications that users' online networking patterns simply reflect their offline networks. There is mild homophily amongst users who have similarly limited offline networks, but increased diversity in political perspectives for users who do not; this results in 'supportive networks' (which could become echo chambers or filter bubbles) as well as 'contrarian clubs' (which fundamentally counteract homophilous tendencies) amongst these *Twitter* users. The research concludes that 'the extent to which social media functions as an echo chamber (as opposed to a contrarian club) varies across individuals' (Vaccari et al. 2016: 8) and is not predetermined by technological features.

Such divergent results also highlight the limits of survey-based and small-scale observational studies, however. If patterns in seeking or avoiding similarity are individual rather than universal, studies of select connective and communicative contexts (pages on *Facebook* or hashtags on *Twitter*) cannot evaluate the balance between 'supportive networks' and 'contrarian clubs' at national or global scales and thereby assess the extent to which users are captured in echo chambers or filter bubbles. On the evidence so far, such enclosure may affect only the most hyperpartisan supporters of extremist movements like the AfD, whose online and offline networks are limited to like-minded ideologues; its extension into mainstream society is prevented by the context collapse that general-purpose social media platforms facilitate and even promote.

Any full assessment is frustrated by the lack of network-scale data on connection and communication patterns on the major platforms, but a handful of studies do explore such larger structures. In Bruns et al. (2017), we presented a first comprehensive mapping and analysis of networks amongst hundreds of thousands of accounts in the Australian Twittersphere: we identified all identifiably Australian *Twitter* profiles then in existence, assessed their follower/followee connections, and applied network analytics to identify clusters of especially dense connectivity. We also collected the accounts' tweets over several years, to correlate the network of *connections* (testing for echo chambers) with the network of *communication* (searching for filter bubbles) between these accounts (Bruns 2017).

The results are instructive: in the follower networks we found clear evidence of clustering around shared topics and interests – for instance around teen culture, sport, and politics. Such broad topical clusters further subdivided into more defined interests (specific sports, particular ideological orientations), but these clusters and subclusters always also retained substantial connections to the wider network; they showed only moderate preference for homophilous attachment to like-minded others (Bruns et al. 2017). In other words, while follower connections clearly reveal distinct communities of interest, their tendency to seek out similarity did not combine with an equivalent desire to avoid difference.

These clusters did not constitute echo chambers – not even for inherently political interests and identities. In particular, accounts from almost any cluster still followed various generic accounts, including mainstream news and media, leading politicians, celebrities, sports stars, utility services, and government agencies.

Moderate preferential attachment through follower *connections* also did not result in significant exclusionary tendencies in day-to-day *communication*. Over the long term, *Twitter* accounts were only mildly more likely to @mention and retweet others in the same cluster and also engaged with many others outside of their immediate network neighbourhood (Bruns 2017). Most clusters retweeted more outside content but kept @mentions more internal; this inserts retweeted material into discussions within the immediate community of interest. The pattern was reversed for politics clusters: here, users retweeted more internal content and @mentioned more external accounts. This amplifies ideas that originated within the more ideologically homogeneous local network by retweeting them across the wider Twittersphere. But whether importing ideas into or exporting views from the local cluster, in either case these clusters clearly do not constitute filter bubbles in any meaningful definition: information *is* flowing readily across the very loosely demarcated boundaries of these communities, and it is highly unlikely that any participant in these flows would be enclosed in an information cocoon.

The fact that generic, multi-purpose platforms such as *Facebook* and *Twitter* are not primarily built around users' political interests is an obvious reason for such cross-cutting network structures. 'A notable proportion of users simply don't pay much attention to the political characteristics of the people in their networks' (Duggan and Smith 2016: 9). Even if they do know about their connections' political preferences, this still does not mean that such knowledge is a determining factor in decisions to friend or follow another user: contrary to Pariser's assumption, we do *not* choose our connections simply because they are 'political compadres'. Amidst growing political acrimony, users might wish to seek solace in more ideologically homogeneous information cocoons by disconnecting from those with opposing ideologies, but the familial, social, or professional penalties that result from creating such ruptures in one's social network act as a significant deterrent: even during the 2016 US presidential election, fewer than one third of users muted, blocked, or unfriended others for political reasons (Duggan and Smith 2016: 4). Much as in offline social circles, in online social media, too, it is difficult to detach from one's uncle, school

"Generic, multi-purpose platforms such as *Facebook* and *Twitter* are not primarily built around users' political interests."

friend, or co-worker just because they express unpalatable political views. Multi-purpose social networks are therefore unlikely to encourage hermetically sealed echo chambers and filter bubbles defined by shared political partisanship; instead, social media turn out to be powerful engines of context collapse. Users have had to accept this fact – and despite the occasional cognitive dissonance, their information diets even benefit substantially.

Although much recent research investigates social media, older notions of filter bubbles as resulting from search and personalisation algorithms have also been challenged. Haim et al. (2018) tested *Google News* by establishing a small number of fake user profiles with different thematic interests, expressed both explicitly through personalisation settings and implicitly through simulated search and browsing histories; after initial training they used each profile to query identical terms and assessed differences in search results. The study found minor or no effects on the diversity of content and sources in search results (Haim et al. 2018: 339).

Exploring similar questions, Nechushtai and Lewis (2019) asked some 168 real users of varying political interest, ideology and geographic location across the

United States to search *Google News* for the major candidates during the 2016 US presidential election; they, too, found only limited evidence of search result personalisation and 'neither ideological bias nor geographic bias' regardless of user demographics (2019: 301). Indeed, one concern they raise is not that *Google News* search results are so divergent that they create distinct and isolated Republican and Democrat filter bubbles, but rather that they are so similar that they lack ideological variety, creating a single national information cocoon, centred on five major news outlets, that encapsulates almost all Americans – 'despite the platform's algorithmic capability of constructing a much more diverse and/or tailored news experience' (Nechushtai and Lewis 2019: 302).

Google News mainly appears to perpetuate long-established positions of market dominance inherited from a pre-digital era (Nechushtai and Lewis 2019: 302), and the researchers come close to suggesting that a *greater* level of personalisation and diversity in search results may be desirable. Unexpectedly, like the German *Facebook* study, these findings almost point to the re-emergence of a unified public sphere, thought to have been fragmented beyond repair by cable TV and the World Wide Web – though we must remember that *Google News* is not the only news aggregator available to those who predominantly seek news through online channels.

This significant concentration of search results on a handful of sources closely matches the highly concentrated patterns of news consumption from 'a small number of relatively centrist sites' that Gentzkow and Shapiro found for US online news consumers in an earlier study (2011: 1801). Do search results observed in 2016 exhibit limited variety because search engine algorithms have learnt to cater to largely centrist user preferences established previously, or do the preferences observed in 2011 already result from *Google*'s algorithmic prioritisation of mainstream news? Perhaps user selections and algorithmic shaping co-evolved together into a feedback loop that reinforces the privileged position of centrist news. Either way, these studies show no evidence of ideological segregation; in Gentzkow and Shapiro's study, the more 'ideologically extreme' sites accounted 'for a very small share of online consumption' (2011: 1802).

Finally, a third study of both *Google News* and *Google Search* recommendations, conducted by Algorithm Watch ahead of the 2017 German federal election (Krafft et al. 2018), harvested data from over 1,500 volunteers who installed a browser plugin that regularly searched both sites for a fixed list of political leaders and parties. This study documents a similar universality of search results in Germany: two randomly chosen volunteers searching simultaneously for the same term would probably have seen the same results – in 5–10% of all cases 'even in the same order' (Krafft et al. 2018: 30; my translation). The picture differs only for volunteers outside of Germany or using a different language: for them, *Google Search* and *Google News* would return more results in the language or from the country that the algorithm assumed for these users; presumably, however, users with the same foreign language or location would yet again experience a considerable overlap in search results.

The empirical observations of these studies, conducted at different scales, in different countries, and in different political contexts, clearly disprove Eli Pariser's foundational hypothesis that search results are so highly personalised that they place users with divergent personal interests and attributes into different filter bubbles. Haim et al. conclude that 'the filter-bubble phenomenon may be overestimated', at least for the algorithmic personalisation of *Google News* results (2018: 339). Algorithm Watch similarly reaches 'the clear conclusion that . . . we can deny the algorithmically based development and solidification of isolating filter bubbles' (Krafft et al. 2018: 53; my translation).

At least as it applies to search personalisation, Pariser's hypothesis, based on very limited anecdotal observations, does not survive rigorous empirical verification.

Overall, then, the more carefully researchers have pursued echo chambers and filter bubbles, the more elusive these structures have become. One explanation for this is a lack of user sophistication: 'perhaps people are simply not very good at controlling what they encounter online', as more advanced customisation features are often complex and inaccessible (Garrett 2009a: 266). Alternatively, users may simply lack motivation to customise their online experiences beyond the default settings: if the preset options are adequate, why waste time on greater personalisation? But there are other explanations beyond a mere lack of interest, too.

The major factors commonly proposed as drivers of echo chambers and filter bubbles are 'homophily and selective exposure' (Batorski and Grzywińska 2018: 359). Both, however, may operate differently from how they are intuitively understood. First, selective exposure theory usually suggests that we avoid new information that refutes our existing attitudes and seek out information that supports them, in order to avoid the cognitive dissonance created by a challenge to our opinions. But such avoidance is not always equally intense, especially when the object of avoidance is less distinct than an obviously unacceptable ideology or deeply disliked political candidate (Brundidge 2010: 683). Indeed, in some contexts it is valuable to be aware of counter-attitudinal information even if one does not agree with it (Garrett et al. 2013: 116).

Therefore, reinforcement-seeking and challenge-avoidance are not necessarily linked: partisans prefer like-minded news sources, but do not avoid 'disagreeable information' (Weeks et al. 2016: 263). The findings of the *Digital News Report* support this perspective: three-quarters of its survey respondents say that search and social media lead them 'to brands they would not otherwise use' (Newman et al. 2015: 16). In other words, the choice between supportive and critical news outlets is no zero-sum calculation, but rather increases the overall volume and range of news that individual users consume – especially as online media enable ready access to a multitude of sources (Garrett 2009b: 676).

While partisans will certainly seek selective *exposure* to like-minded sources of news and information, 'there is simply no evidence for selective avoidance or partisan "echo chambers"' (Weeks et al. 2016: 263). Some individuals deliberately monitor both those alternative news outlets they agree with and the mainstream publications where they also encounter contrary views (Garrett et al. 2013: 114). They also follow counter-attitudinal accounts, hashtags, or pages in full anticipation that they will disagree with their views (known in extreme cases as 'hate-following'). This way, users inoculate themselves against the views they encounter there and reinforce their sense of the superiority of their own perspectives. Some users also actively engage and argue against such views (occasionally turning into all-out flaming and trolling). These practices are personally and socially disruptive, but they certainly do not produce exclusionary connection and communication practices – their effect is quite the opposite, in fact.

In addition to selective exposure at the informational level, the second proposed mechanism in the formation of echo chambers and filter bubbles is homophily at the interpersonal level. In particular, since evidence for the significant algorithmic effects he had anticipated has remained elusive, Eli Pariser himself has shifted to highlighting homophilous tendencies as a cause of filter bubbles: he now claims that 'who you're friends with matters a good deal more than the algorithm' (Pariser 2015: n.p.). But as we have seen, homophily too may be overrated, especially in generic social media platforms like *Facebook* and *Twitter*: here, the various purposes to which such platforms are put counteract the force of homophilous attraction in any one specific context.

Even an overall affinity in interests within an online community does not inevitably translate into strong homophily: generally like-minded online communities still experience spirited and acrimonious in-group debates (Yardi and boyd 2010: 326).

If, following Pariser, homophily were the mechanism drawing users into ideologically orthodox filter bubbles, this could happen only if a user made all decisions on connecting and communicating with others solely based on shared political identity; this is likely only for exceptionally committed partisans who will readily unfriend even their family, friends, co-workers, and other close acquaintances for expressing impure political perspectives. Ordinary, real-life users – indeed, ordinary, real-life *people*, on social media or elsewhere – tend to be considerably more complex, far from this one-dimensional caricature of 'political compadres'; they variously suffer or benefit from substantial context collapse in their social networks, encountering unexpected views and ideas whether they want it or not. Indeed, because they are less tied to geography, online networks may be especially diverse (Vriens and van Ingen 2018: 2436). Further, by their very existence – and if they so choose, also by their actions – users who experience such context collapse also actively contribute to it: 'each person who is a member of more than one network connects or bridges them' (O'Hara and Stevens 2015: 413; cf. Messing and Westwood 2014: 1045).

In our online social networks, then, we might *feel* amongst like-minded individuals, embedded in homophilous networks (as Pariser assumes), but empirical reality challenges this intuition. This reality becomes clearer around politics: during the 2016 US presidential election, for instance, 64% of respondents to a Pew Center survey said that 'their online encounters with people on the opposite side of the political spectrum leave them feeling as if they have even less in common than they thought' (Duggan and Smith 2016: 3). Realistically, then, in our social media environments we are simultaneously part of various more or less strongly homophilous networks – but these networks overlap only imperfectly and indeed often pull us in diametrically opposed directions, counteracting the potential echo chamber or filter bubble tendencies that each single homophilous network in isolation might promote.

If the power of selective exposure and homophilous attachment is overrated, this is in part because they are both counteracted by the sheer messiness of empirical reality. This messiness manifests especially in the form of serendipitous exposure: our networks are heterogeneous and our contacts in these networks are far from consistent in the content they post, like, retweet, comment on, or share, so we constantly encounter unexpected and unpredictable views and ideas. As Helberger remarks, 'even Sunstein concedes that unexpected exposures may help to "promote understanding" and open-mindedness, and thereby also advance democratic goals' (2011: 454) – but Sunstein and other proponents of the echo chamber and filter bubble thesis fail to recognise that the power of such very human inconsistencies is far greater than the capacity of personal preferences or platform algorithms to channel them into a topically or ideologically consistent stream of information.

This is because organised politics and political news generally are a very minor interest in most people's lives (Newman et al. 2015: 14). Instead, users encounter political issues as an adjunct to their immediate interests: users of 'an online breast cancer support group . . . may inadvertently be exposed to a heterogeneous political discussion on the US healthcare system' (Brundidge 2010: 685). Contrary to explicitly political online spaces, however, such groups are not organised along partisan lines and therefore provide much greater opportunity for open and cross-ideological exchanges between users who otherwise have the same interests. This assigns particular importance to the role of 'casual political talk online' in overcoming ideological divides (Wojcieszak and Mutz 2009: 50); such everyday political talk is documented across various national and topical contexts (e.g. Duggan and Smith 2016: 6; Schmidt et al. 2017: 76). Such serendipitous encounters also improve the information diets of users, by introducing a greater diversity of online news sources (Fletcher and Nielsen 2018: 2459).

As social media users are thus serendipitously and inadvertently exposed to diverse news and political content from varying ideological perspectives, the fact that this content reaches them through their immediate network of family, friends, and other acquaintances also means that they pay more attention to it than to generic news reports or political statements (Messing and Westwood 2014: 1043); this is the case even for individuals who otherwise avoid political content (Anspach 2017: 591). Experimental studies suggest that such social endorsements can overcome ideological preferences: individuals engage with material that challenges their own politics if it is endorsed strongly enough by their social networks (Messing and Westwood 2014: 1056; Anspach 2017: 591). In part, this may be because social media platforms emphasise social cues (who shared a news article) over institutional provenance (who published the article).

This holds especially for those who are traditionally least exposed to news and political content – especially 'including women and younger groups', as the 2015 *Digital News Report* highlights (Newman et al. 2015: 16). Other such audiences include users of lower socioeconomic status, and ethnic and other minorities (Newman et al. 2015: 77; Mitchell et al. 2016: 7). Such increased exposure to news and political discussion actively works against any communicative isolation that these groups may traditionally have experienced, potentially empowering them to claim a greater share of the online conversation for themselves (Yardi and boyd 2010: 325).

Viewed in this light, contemporary social media still strongly resemble the offline social networks studied by pioneering researchers such as Paul Lazarsfeld and Elihu Katz in the 1940s and 1950s; then as now, we observe processes of opinion leadership and two- or multi-step flows of information between more and less well-informed members of the network (Anspach 2017: 594). 'It is remarkable how well the theory agrees with our observations', write Wu et al. (2011: 711) – but as we deal here with fundamental dynamics in human communication, independent of specific media platforms and channels used to communicate, perhaps we need not be especially surprised. Rather, to assume that, for all their novel approaches to the mediation and algorithmisation of such communication, *Facebook* or *Twitter* would significantly alter these fundamental dynamics is to fall prey to technological determinism; in the main, they simply appear to make serendipitous encounters with counter-attitudinal content more common.

Indeed, apparently the reverse also holds: an absence of opportunities to connect online results in an increase in ideological isolation. Using long-term demographic information from the United States, Boxell et al. report that populations on the wrong side of the digital divide 'experienced larger changes in polarization between 1996 and 2016 than the groups most likely to use the Internet' (2017: 10612). Remarkably, this reverses completely the assumption promoted by followers of Sunstein and Pariser (and adopted by Obama) that the Internet and social media fragment society and allow supporters of different worldviews to disappear into their separate information cocoons. Instead, those *least* connected through online media are also least familiar with alternative ideological perspectives.

This bird's-eye demographic perspective helps to highlight that individual social media platforms do not exist in isolation, but are part of a much wider mediasphere and of the 'diverse media repertoires of citizens'

(Thorson and Wells 2016: 320). These repertoires take in online and offline media: face-to-face communication, print, radio, television, mainstream and alternative news websites, search, social media, mobile apps, even voice-controlled virtual assistants. In this complex, multifaceted, and continuously transforming jumble of platforms, networks, sources, and participants, an observation of activities on any single platform, even if it were comprehensive, is insufficient for fully tracing information flows. Instead, 'it is important to consider the entire range of media individuals use in this high-choice media environment' (Dubois and Blank 2018a: 730).

Further, even within single platforms we might observe inherently contrary processes. On the one hand, *Facebook* pages can serve as engines of homophily, as they do for the extremist followers of Germany's AfD. On the other, *Facebook* profiles are engines of context collapse, as serendipitous news exposure itself and complaints about such exposure to unwanted political views both demonstrate. Whether social media facilitate greater ideological segregation or increased exposure to diversity therefore relates directly to the media literacies and usage strategies of individual participants. Studies that seek to determine once and for all whether a given platform supports an inclusive public sphere or divisive echo chambers are therefore condemned to defeat: 'the answer is that this depends' (Colleoni et al. 2014: 328).

As robust empirical evidence against the echo chamber and filter bubble thesis has grown, scholars have taken an increasingly sceptical stance towards these concepts. As Garrett notes, 'people have not abandoned the main-stream media for more partisan alternatives, as Sunstein suggests they might' if they were drifting off into echo chambers (2009b: 694); Zuiderveen Borgesius et al. are similarly adamant that 'at present there is little empirical evidence that warrants any worries about filter bubbles' (2016: 1). It seems especially unlikely that anybody could lock themselves into a hermetically sealed echo chamber or filter bubble *across* the multiple media platforms that constitute our contemporary media environment (Dubois and Blank 2018a: 730); this may not be entirely impossible, and easier for people in areas with poor media diversity and Internet connectivity, but the effort required would overwhelm all but the most committed ideologues.

To illustrate the considerable detachment from observable reality that underpins the echo chamber and filter bubble myths, let us conclude this chapter with a brief thought experiment: to build ourselves an information cocoon to share with fellow partisans, how exactly would we have to go about it? First, we would have to 'cut off communications from heterodox sources while providing good connections to orthodox adherents' (O'Hara 2014: 80). This would require extreme homophily, coupled with equally extreme heterophobia, of ourselves and our fellow travellers: severing any existing contacts to non-adherents, online and offline, through which outside views could reach us, much as 'people are adopted into cults, brainwashed, and alienated from their contacts' (O'Hara and Stevens 2015: 416). No easy task.

We could aid our isolation by limiting our media use to just a handful of channels and platforms – ideally niche rather than general-purpose spaces to avoid context collapse. In more generic platforms, we would use only select affordances: for instance, closed and carefully controlled *Facebook* groups, but not public pages or other users' profiles. But to maintain this detachment day-to-day would be difficult: interference from the platforms' own tracking and recommendation algorithms might result in inadvertent exposure to unwanted ideas. All members of our clique would need to exercise exceptional discipline in our connective and communicative practices, also in order to train search and social algorithms to only produce appropriate and ideologically acceptable results.

Longer-term persistence with these activity patterns at a level sufficient to produce 'hard', truly exclusive echo chambers and filter bubbles would be exceptionally time-consuming and labour-intensive. Perhaps individual users could succeed; that they could do so *en masse* seems extremely unlikely, however – as O'Hara and Stevens (2015) state, their ideological vigilance would have to reach practically cultish levels. Some such cults may indeed exist, motivated by an intense fervour for one or hatred towards another side of politics: the small groups of highly active 'fake news' sharers during the 2016 US presidential election that Guess et al. (2018) found may meet this description. Yet even these hardcore ideologues were not necessarily disconnected from mainstream media exposure: as hyperpartisans, they took an intensely oppositional stance towards such media, but nonetheless monitored them for intelligence on the issues and developments to which they could attach new disinformation.

To be sure, we might achieve considerable levels of preferential, homophilous attachment to like-minded others within specific spaces and in particular contexts; such choices in users' media repertoires do affect their information diets to a certain extent, and these effects could be measured as a *degree* of disconnection. But ultimately these effects remain weak and the enclosure remains porous: this is not the information cocoon fragmenting our society and democracy that Sunstein, Pariser, and even Obama warned of. Such porous echo chambers and filter bubbles are little more than the network clusters we saw in the Australian Twittersphere: communities of interest that accumulate around shared topics and identities, but do not detach altogether from the world beyond. 'No one would be trapped by the technology without hope of relief' (O'Hara and Stevens 2015: 414).

'This, then, 'is the myth of the filter bubble' – or echo chamber – 'that allegedly radicalises people and divides society, that made Donald Trump, the AfD, and Brexit possible in the first place. But most of all this myth is one thing: a big misunderstanding' (Meineck 2018: n.p.; my translation). It is a misunderstanding especially about the power of technology – and in particular, of algorithms – over human communication: a power that is strong in specific spaces on particular platforms, but that is considerably less irresistible than the proponents of these myths would have us believe. As O'Hara and Stevens observe, 'the echo chamber argument seems to suggest that technology is a homogeneous influence on an individual whose social context is, if not fixed, at least not particularly multidimensional. Yet this does not accord with experience' (2015: 412). As a long history of media and cultural studies inquiry has made abundantly clear, we each have multiple identities, which we perform according to the social contexts we find ourselves in – and, especially in online and social media environments, those contexts are more and more often collapsing onto one another.

FIVE

Conclusion:
Polarised but Not Disconnected

Echo chambers and filter bubbles are exceptionally attractive concepts; they offer a simple, technological explanation for problems that many emerging and established democracies face. However, the closer one looks and the more one attempts to detect them in observable reality, the more outlandish and unrealistic they appear. The images of 'chambers' and 'bubbles' conjure up hermetically sealed spaces where only politically like-minded participants connect and only ideologically orthodox information circulates, but this seems highly improbable; Meineck therefore goes as far as calling filter bubbles 'the dumbest metaphor of the Internet' (2018: n.p.; my translation).

The research we have encountered shows simply no empirical evidence for these information cocoons in their absolute definitions, especially in a complex, multi-platform environment. As Dubois and Blank summarise it, whatever may be happening on any single social media platform, when we look at the entire media environment, there is little apparent echo chamber. People regularly encounter things that they disagree with. People check multiple sources. People try to confirm information using search. Possibly most important, people discover things that change their political opinions. Looking at the entire multi-media environment, we find little evidence of an echo chamber. (2018a: 740)

Yes, selective exposure and homophily do exist; there would be no political parties, activist movements, interest communities, fan groups, sports clubs, or other social institutions without them. But contrary to the dark visions of Sunstein, Pariser, and others who see echo chambers and filter bubbles as engines of social, political and societal fragmentation, a preference for particular ideas, values, and beliefs does not inevitably lead to the exclusion of anybody who holds different views, or the disconnection from information sources that present those views: we cluster, but we do not segregate.

Mainly, the debate about these concepts and their apparent impacts on society and democracy constitutes a moral panic. Social commentators have always been quick to jump to conclusions about new media technologies and to compare the technologically remediated present to a mythical golden era when political and societal participation seemed simpler and more direct. This obsession with ideal types of political engagement obscures the question of whether the *actual* uses people make of online and social media today have a net positive or net negative effect on political processes, or whether indeed the positives and negatives that different groups experience cancel each other out in the end (Fletcher and Nielsen 2018: 2453).

Only a small substrate of political extremists seem so committed to their cause that they diverge notably from the societal mainstream; hardcore supporters of the neo-fascist AfD party in Germany are one example, and their disconnect from and hatred for the mainstream and its political and journalistic institutions should certainly concern us. However, to attack it more effectively, even they must monitor what they hate: they are hyperpartisan and polarised, but do not live in hermetically sealed information cocoons. Maintaining ideological segregation is difficult and time-consuming, and partisans must be exceptionally motivated to do so. Consequently, 'Sunstein's prediction that people will take any opportunity to screen out other perspectives seems unnecessarily grave' (Garrett 2009b: 694), even for fringe groups.

Ironically, echo chamber and filter bubble concepts may have become so popular with some journalists, media critics, and politicians because members of these professional classes *are* genuinely more likely to inhabit an information cocoon of sorts. High-profile journalists do tend to remain in a 'journalism-centered bubble' (Nuernbergk 2016: 877); theirs is an intensely selective, high-pressure workplace that takes them away from everyday social interactions and sequesters them inside parliamentary press corps which often lack socio-economic, ethnic, and even gender diversity. (The same applies to politicians and their staff, at least at the national level.)

But a disenchantment with the 'inside the beltway' journalism of horse-race politics and political point-scoring is now widespread precisely because ordinary citizens do not inhabit the professional cocoons that enclose the political classes: this form of journalism and politics fails to address their own lived experiences. Such disenchantment results not only in populist calls to 'drain the swamp' and replace one form of political myopia with another, more extreme one; in mainstream society, it also creates an unfulfilled demand to reform political systems so that they focus less on fighting symbolic ideological battles and more on finding consensus on the right policies to improve citizens' lives. These demands, too, are expressed through social media, where they are directed at the journalists and politicians themselves. Although the political classes have long had a tendency to talk predominantly amongst themselves, they are therefore now also exposed to considerably more, and considerably more *public*, criticism than ever before – if they choose to pay attention. Social media make politics 'a conversation that can be joined by outsiders' (Ausserhofer and Maireder 2013: 306).

Overall, then, generic social media platforms like *Facebook* and *Twitter* break down more barriers than they erect – they are important engines of context collapse, rather than enablers of ideological segregation. They help (or force) us to maintain at least a passive, ambient awareness (Hermida 2010) of how 'the other side' thinks; we might even actively seek out such information – not necessarily to be persuaded by it, but perhaps to inoculate ourselves against its rhetoric. This is true even (and perhaps especially) for people with fringe views: even visitors to extreme white supremacist sites visit mainstream outlets such as the *New York Times*, and indeed do so more often than mainstream users (Gentzkow and Shapiro 2011: 1823). They might read established media only to better counter mainstream coverage by presenting 'alternative facts' of their own – but they do read them.

Although the spectrum of sources from the extreme fringe to the *New York Times* and beyond demonstrates that, from an information *supply* perspective, 'we are well on the road to segmentation' (Katz 1996: 23), then, on the information *demand* side considerably more overlap remains. There is 'no support for the idea that online audiences are more fragmented than offline audiences' (Fletcher and Nielsen 2017: 476); the *Daily Me* that Negroponte envisaged in 1995, and the extreme diversification of personal information diets that was expected to follow, have not arrived. For all the legitimate concern over the mysterious ways in which they operate, the algorithms of search and social media platforms may be partly responsible for this: they also identify the interests and trends common to everyone's online activities. Consequently, online and offline media diets remain 'characterized by a surprisingly high degree of overlap underneath a veneer of fragmentation' (Fletcher and Nielsen 2017: 491).

To combat whatever level of fragmentation still remains, and to ward off any danger of sliding into echo chamber and filter bubble enclosures after all, various solutions have been proposed. Some activists – including Eli Pariser himself – suggest that people could 'sabotage personalization systems' by meddling with user tracking systems, varying the search engines they use, or even searching for and liking random content (Bozdag and van den Hoven 2015: 254). However, in light of the very limited impact of personalisation in search and other contexts, such measures seem like overkill; they are 'not only tedious, but . . . bad for the user as well' (Bozdag and van den Hoven 2015: 254), as they also undermine some genuine benefits of personalisation. To fully avoid personalisation would seem as difficult and time-consuming as it is to deliberately build an information cocoon around a group of like-minded partisans.

A more sensible alternative may be to adjust the affordances and logics of contemporary online and social media platforms to ensure that they present a balanced information diet even for users with singularly limited interests. If there is an upside to the moral panic about echo chambers and filter bubbles, then it is the momentum to explore such adjustments that it has created. 'Diversity by design' (Helberger 2011) could give special prominence to the views of minorities, focus more on highlighting important stories, offer better platforms for political debate, ensure the widespread distribution of breaking news, explain the choices made by algorithmic selection, and provide diverse rather than just popular perspectives (Bozdag and Hoven 2015: 262). Such goals are easy to formulate, but considerably more difficult to implement in any meaningful and reliably effective way. Which minorities? Which alternative views? How far should they be allowed to diverge from mainstream perspectives? After all, journalism itself already does some of this, without algorithms, but through its pursuit of all sides of an argument we also end up with a false equivalence between the overwhelming scientific evidence for climate change and the far-fetched conspiracy theories of climate change denialists.

Such diversity by design would need implementation at the platform level, by the search engines and social media sites themselves. A different approach would send independent automated agents to roam the social networks and to undo and reverse tendencies towards homophily and selective exposure. Graham and Ackland describe two possible models for such agents: their 'popperbot' would infiltrate segments of social media networks that exhibit especially high levels of homophily and '"inject" information reflecting more moderate or even contrasting ideological standpoints' to pop these filter bubbles (2017: 199); alternatively, a 'bridgerbot' could circulate information between opposing homophilous clusters, by 'tweeting/retweeting and following users from both "sides" of a given political or ideological debate' and thus bridging the disconnects between them (2017: 201).

Such concepts are well-intentioned and honourable, but they could aim at the wrong targets, make inappropriate interventions, and eventually cause more harm than good. These direct interventions represent a form of 'nudging' that O'Hara and Stevens describe as 'stealthy paternalism' (2015: 417): like other forms of intervention by well-meaning outsiders, they may cement their target groups' opposition to the mainstream rather than open them up to new perspectives. The greater exposure to diverse perspectives that popper- and bridgerbots would facilitate could backfire by leading to increased polarisation (cf. Bail et al. 2018).

For some communities, such bots might even have destructive consequences: in pursuing a 'diversity of opinions', they could just as easily push homophobic content into communities of LGBTIQ+ users as they might promote tolerance in communities of homophobes. From the bot's point of view, these actions are equivalent: they reduce homophily and expose community members to new views. From a human point of view, only one is socially acceptable and beneficial. Ultimately, this highlights the fact that such interventions (through automated or manual means) are not value-neutral: their designers, operators, algorithms, and bots implement moral and political choices. The idea that echo chamber and filter bubble tendencies could be reduced by technological means simply perpetuates the deterministic myth that digital technologies caused them in the first place (Meineck 2018).

One further approach to combatting information cocoons is technological in essence, too, because it would be implemented largely through technological means: new laws and regulations that promote and ensure more diverse media consumption by the users of search engines and social media platforms. Such initiatives often seek to translate media diversity rules from offline to online environments, but struggle with the considerably different structures and affordances of search engines and social media (Helberger 2018: 166). This is not an argument against regulation itself: there are opportunities for improvements to the operation of search engines and social media platforms, but to assess the practical impact of regulatory interventions on the information diets of everyday users is far from trivial.

Finally, for any technological, regulatory, and legislative interventions, a fundamental question remains: which platforms should they address? Should they focus only on *Facebook* and other leading providers or also address niche and emergent sites? What about mobile instant-messaging services, whose communicative affordances are unlike those of their Web-based predecessors? As the mix of popular platforms changes, can and will regulations keep up, especially if we still lack sufficient empirical evidence on the connection and communication patterns typical for such platforms? There is a considerable danger that new legislation will adopt a highly simplistic, empirically unsupported view of echo chambers and filter bubbles and thereby address an abstract moral panic rather than the reality of everyday online and social media use.

Indeed, the moral panic about such information cocoons obscures a far more serious and far more real threat to society and democracy. David Weinberger once remarked, 'the problem with an extraterrestrial-conspiracy mailing list isn't that it's an echo chamber; it's that it thinks there's a conspiracy by extraterrestrials' (2004: n.p.); today, the problem in online and offline communication is not that citizens are sealed into hyperpartisan and extremist echo chambers or filter bubbles, but that too many citizens hold hyperpartisan and extremist views. The problem, in short, is *polarisation*, not *fragmentation*, and such polarisation is not the result of our use of online and social media platforms. Rather, many of the well-known causes of polarisation still persist: for example, socioeconomic inequalities, citizen disenfranchisement, and inflammatory political propaganda (Beam et al. 2018b: 953).

The distinction between fragmentation and polarisation may appear slight, but is nonetheless crucial. Fragmentation implies the existence of echo chambers and filter bubbles, where like-minded partisans connect and communicate amongst themselves and are oblivious to the views of the outside world. But this manifestly does not represent contemporary experience. Rather, as citizens especially on the fringes of the political spectrum become more polarised in their worldviews, they still *hear* but are increasingly less willing to *listen to* the views of their political opponents, preferring instead to repeat their own beliefs ever more noisily. Social media certainly do provide a forum for this, by enabling these extremists to amplify each other's voices and coordinate their activities more efficiently, but they are not the root cause of such developments (Meineck 2018).

Indeed, our considerable focus on the alleged deleterious effects of echo chambers and filter bubbles since Sunstein introduced his concept in 2001 and Pariser followed suit in 2011, and the widespread portrayal of these dysfunctions as having technological origins and therefore also requiring technological solutions, has produced the perverse effect that far less attention has been paid to the human causes of polarisation and their very real and alarming impacts on society and democracy. The problem is 'that these people are feeling hatred and mistrust at all' (Meineck 2018: n.p.; my translation); it is this social and societal challenge that we must urgently confront, rather than continuing to chase the mirage of echo chambers and filter bubbles.

Participants in hyperpartisan communities are often highly homogeneous in their attitudes and identities and 'even ignore facts that would prove their arguments wrong' (Spohr 2017: 151). Indeed, they are not only resistant to divergent perspectives, but actively combat them by aggressively (and often successfully) pushing their own views into wider public debate; during the 2016 US presidential election, the hyperpartisan 'pro-Trump media sphere' not only led the conservative media agenda, 'but also strongly influenced the broader media agenda, in particular coverage of Hillary Clinton' (Benkler et al. 2017: 1). These groups even shared untruths in full knowledge that they were 'fake news', because they knew that subsequent media coverage would hurt their political opponents' public standing and annoy opposition supporters.

Indeed, for populist movements that seek to do more than agitate from the sidelines, any voluntary seclusion into echo chambers and filter bubbles is self-evidently counter-productive: they are inherently interested in establishing a strong public presence and convincing more moderate citizens of their populist message, drawing them gradually towards the hyperpartisan and extremist fold (Krämer 2017: 1302). These populist agitators actively exploit the very *absence* of echo chambers and filter bubbles in everyday online communication: drawing on human and automated means, they attempt to engineer widespread social endorsement and sharing of their populist messages (including the deliberate misrepresentations and falsehoods included under the problematic label 'fake news') to ensure that these messages travel far beyond the partisan in-group of the already converted. This way, they abuse the connective and communicative affordances of *Facebook* and other platforms to trick social media users into greater exposure to partisan content, even though most have a very limited interest in politics by default (Anspach 2017: 602).

Such attempts at converting new recruits are not always successful, of course: as social media users encounter populist messages, it is possible and perhaps even likely that they have already developed the media literacy to critically evaluate these messages. Here, those users who are politically active and have therefore formed a pre-existing ideological perspective are least susceptible to populist messaging: during the presidential election of 2016, for instance, politically active social media users in the United States were less likely to support Donald Trump, while those with a more passing interest in politics were easier targets for his propaganda (Groshek and Koc-Michalska 2017: 1397). Further, interest in populist messages might also be temporary, and true, long-term contagion is complex and slow rather than simple and rapid: 'in a world of constant distractions, with intense competition for limited attention, even key events can break through only temporarily' (Guess 2016: 29).

Even an only gradual spread of populist and hyperpartisan messages across society is nonetheless a significant cause for concern, not least when it actively employs misinformation and outright falsehoods. Unfortunately, effective countermeasures for combatting populism and extremism in the contemporary media environment still remain unclear: for instance, fact-checking and rumour-debunking initiatives are often ignored by their principal targets. 'Attempts to convince conspiracists that their beliefs are false generally seem to fail' (Quattrociocchi et al. 2016: 14), not least because hyperpartisan groups anticipate these attempts and see them as further evidence that 'the establishment' opposes them and that their own views must therefore be justified. Hostile reactions by the mainstream only 'confirm one's status as a critical outsider' (Krämer 2017: 1302).

Fact-checking services are nonetheless useful and should be maintained, of course; they do also serve to inoculate media users with more mainstream views against the extremist messages they debunk, and help those who are wavering between mainstream and populist views to encounter another side of the argument. Indeed, mainstream media may need to react more strongly and immediately against falsehoods rather than afford them equal space in coverage at first and then debunk them later, when they have already been disseminated widely. A journalism that provides equal space to mainstream and extremist arguments out of a misunderstood sense of 'fairness' or 'balance' creates false equivalence between them and serves to normalise political extremism by making it appear like just another voice on the political spectrum.

None of these challenges are especially new: how journalism, politics, and society should deal with the threat from populism and other forms of extremism has been debated in the age of newspapers, radio, and television as much as in the age of search and social media. Our challenge now is to learn from how previous generations have dealt with populism: to avoid their mistakes and to adapt their – predominantly non-technological – solutions to a changed but not entirely different media, political, and societal environment. Most importantly, 'one lesson we should have learned from the past is that panic does not lead to sane policies' (Zuiderveen Borgesius et al. 2016: 11): meaningful interventions must build on a solid and carefully reviewed evidence base.

In addressing these challenges, it will be especially important to remain attentive to local specificities. A great deal more scholarly attention has been directed at the media and political systems and societal contexts of the United States, 'characterised by a bipolar political system' (Zuiderveen Borgesius et al. 2016: 8) and considerable institutional dysfunction, than on the political environments of leading European nations or the widely divergent political systems elsewhere in the world; such US-centric studies offer little help in understanding the dynamics of polarisation in other countries. The agonistic two-party systems prevalent in the United States and some other Anglophone democracies vary considerably from the multi-party, consensus-oriented democracies that are typical elsewhere, and the insurgence of populism has been less successful in many of the latter countries than in the United States or the United Kingdom. Other factors further complicate the picture: diverse and dominant mainstream media – including especially also strong and independent public broadcasting – may serve as a bulwark against populist tendencies, while limited experience with stable democratic governments (for example in the former Soviet bloc) might render citizens more susceptible to the populist promise of strongman autocracy. Finally, as the 2016 US presidential election demonstrates, even long-established democracies may fall prey to persistent interference from political, commercial, and foreign state actors with a shared interest in undermining established conventions, but not all countries have been targeted by actors of bad faith to a similar degree.

One promising way to protect populations from the snake oil of populism is to enable them to protect themselves, by increasing their critical media literacy and thereby equipping them with the tools to spot hyperpartisan biases, falsehoods, and fakes (Dubois and Blank 2018a: 742). Such media literacy initiatives could also aim to generally 'stimulate open-mindedness' and promote tolerance towards different opinions (Helberger 2011: 455). Users of online and social media, in particular, must be empowered not only to identify the biases of the human creators of the content they encounter, but also the biases introduced by the algorithmic filtering and recommendation mechanisms that have shaped these encounters; this is a matter not simply of media literacy, but more specifically of algorithmic literacy (cf. Nielsen 2016: 113). Such literacy should aim to increase the diversity of the media sources that online and social media users engage with and emphasise fact-checking as a fundamental media usage routine (Dubois and Blank 2018b: n.p.).

As Bradshaw puts it in his advice to journalists using social media, our choice of connection and communication partners is similarly crucial – 'designing serendipity into your workflow is now part of what makes a good journalist: curiosity expressed algorithmically. Design your way out of the filter bubble' (2016: n.p.). The point holds for ordinary users as well: as Spohr suggests,

> we as citizens need to be aware that news consumption should be an active process and that ideologically diverse, high-quality news content does not simply find us because we are constantly online and surrounded by information. To have a better informed society, getting political information needs to be a conscious act of seeking out diverse sources and political discussions should be based again on an openness to listen to the other side. (2017: 157)

In light of the startling observation by Boxell et al. (2017) that the least digitally connected segments of the US population have shown the greatest increase in polarisation over the past two decades, however, we should not focus on digital and social media literacy alone. Quite possibly, only a combination of various government, educational, civil society, and commercial initiatives will improve online and offline media, digital, and algorithmic literacy to a point where citizens become more resistant to populist messages.

Sadly, however, there is a significant *caveat* to this argument for media literacy: the very strategies of critical media literacy have also been adopted and weaponised by the merchants of mis- and disinformation themselves. As Starbird points out, these conspiracy theorists, hyperpartisans and populist agitators 'have co-opted arguments about media literacy . . . and critical thinking' (2017a: n.p.) and openly encourage their own followers to question everything, especially when it originates from the mainstream media. This sentiment is echoed every time Donald Trump attacks mainstream news outlets as 'fake news media', too. This way, the very tools designed to inoculate citizens against manipulation by demagogues are now used by these demagogues to inoculate their followers against initiatives that seek to rescue them from the populist fringe. This is no reason to give up on media literacy altogether, but it means that we are locked into an arms race that will continue for the foreseeable future.

As this fight against populist demagoguery continues, however, let us finally put the misleading and obscurantist concepts of echo chambers and filter bubbles to rest; they have well outlived whatever limited use value they had. Yes, it is empirically true that national and international media and political systems, online and social media technologies, the algorithms on which they increasingly depend, and especially also users and their communities, combine to create competing information environments that privilege some and downplay other information, ideas, values, and beliefs (cf. Madsen 2016). But equally, the evidence shows that such information environments do not constitute hermetically sealed echo chambers where only a select in-group connect with each other, or filter bubbles where only ideologically orthodox information is communicated. Rather, these clusters, groups, or communities within the wider social networks enabled by online and social media also interpenetrate each other; the social, topical, and political contexts they represent collapse onto one another; and these online spaces intersect with their users' offline identities and activities in various unexpected ways. To maintain a description of this jumble of overlapping publics as 'chambers' or 'bubbles' stretches these metaphors well beyond their common-sense meanings.

As Meineck puts it, then, such concepts are 'the desperate attempt to make technology responsible for . . . societal problems' (2018: n.p.; my translation). Importantly, their comparative innocence on *this* count does not absolve *Google*, *Facebook*, *Twitter*, and other providers of their responsibility in other critical contexts, though; while their affordances and algorithms do not cause echo chambers and filter bubbles, they do materially affect user experience in other ways that are just as crucial and must be subjected to far greater scrutiny (cf. Koene 2016). These platforms play an ever more critical role as key brokers of information flows in contemporary society: 'processes of opinion formation are no longer imaginable without [these] intermediaries, because they now penetrate information and communication practices in many ways' (Schmidt et al. 2017: 98). With that power, however, also comes great public responsibility, and legislators, regulators, politicians, platform operators, scholars, civil society organisations, and ordinary citizens must determine together how that responsibility should be enforced and exercised.

But we must not rush to legislation. As Weinberger warned as early as 2004, 'the "echo chamber" meme is not only ill-formed, but it also plays into the hands of those who are ready to misconstrue the Net in order to control it. We'd all be better off if we stopped repeating it and let its sound fade' (2004: n.p.). Rather than using poorly thought-through concepts as a justification for radical interference in existing political, commercial, media, or social structures, we need to consider far more calmly and carefully what we seek to achieve through legislative and regulatory means, and what levers are available to us to achieve it.

At the conclusion of this book, then, we arrive at an interesting and unexpected point. The empirical research, drawing on surveys and small-scale observations and on advanced and innovative digital methods and 'big social data', demonstrates clearly that echo chambers and filter bubbles not only do not exist outside the very fringes of mainstream society, but that the incessant and continuing focus of media coverage, media scholarship, and political debate on these ill-defined ideas overemphasises the role of platforms and their algorithms in current political crises, and obscures a far more critical challenge: the return of naked, hyper-partisan populism and political demagoguery.

These populists do not live in isolated information cocoons, but are perhaps even better informed about mainstream views than the ordinary citizens of the mainstream – yet they remain impervious and deeply opposed to moderate perspectives. The reasons for this opposition should not be sought in their communicative preferences: hyperpartisans use many of the same platforms and tools as the societal mainstream. But 'none of the evidence . . . speaks to the way people translate the content they encounter into beliefs' (Gentzkow and Shapiro 2011: 1802): our discussion has reached the outer limits of the useful applicability of observational digital methods research and instead suggests a renewed focus on research into media psychology: the question is no longer what material these hyperpartisans encounter and how much that information diet is shaped by algorithms, but rather how they receive and process this content and incorporate it into their worldviews.

Citizens in the mainstream and at the fringes of political debate each encounter a variety of news and perspectives, accepting the content that agrees with their worldviews and processing the information that does not. 'The sharers of xenophobic fake news do certainly notice how news media debunk these fake news stories', for instance, but find reasons to reject the debunking (Meineck 2018: n.p.; my translation). Conversely, ordinary citizens may encounter the same fake news stories and choose not to share them, yet pass on the content that fact-checks them. What are the

"In a hyperconnected yet deeply polarised world, the most important filter remains in our heads, not in our networks."

psychological processes that place one user in the first and another in the second category? Are they the same in each case and merely acting on diametrically opposed worldviews? And do these patterns apply to all counter-attitudinal content or only the most obvious fake news stories?

As Meineck puts it, 'when the tale of the filter bubble bursts, the debate about the transformation of the public sphere can get started' (2018: n.p.; my translation); that time is now. *This* is the debate we need to be having: not some proxy argument about the impact of platforms and algorithms, but a meaningful discussion about the complex and compound causes of political and societal polarisation. And this is a debate that must involve all of us: governments, politicians, media, journalists, scholars, educators, activists, and ordinary citizens, as we in the mainstream of society confront the renewed challenge of hyperpartisanship, populism, and political extremism together. This requires us to understand the internal calculus, the motivations, the psychology of hyperpartisans as they navigate the complex informational environments they inhabit. These people may indeed be so secure in their ideological convictions that they accept 'only information, whether it's true or not, that fits [their] opinions, instead of basing [their] opinions on the evidence that is out there', as President

Obama suggested in his farewell speech (2017: n.p.) – but they have not enclosed themselves in echo chambers or filter bubbles to achieve such certainty.

Instead, it is evident that even – indeed, perhaps especially – these inhabitants of the most polarised fringes of contemporary society still encounter material that challenges their perspectives and engage with users who represent opposing views. The question is *what they do* with such information when they encounter it: do they dismiss it immediately as running counter to their own received wisdom? Do they engage in a critical reading of this information, turning it into further material to support their own worldview, perhaps as evidence for their own conspiracy theories? Do they respond by offering counter-arguments, by vocally and even violently disagreeing, by making *ad hominem* attacks, or by knowingly disseminating all-out lies as 'alternative facts'? More important yet, *why do they do so*? What is it that has so entrenched and cemented their beliefs that they are no longer open to contestation?

In a hyperconnected yet deeply polarised world, the most important filter remains in our heads, not in our networks: it is the cognitive filter that makes us reject some ideas out of hand, even despite the evidence that supports them, while we cling to others than have long since been disproven and discredited. Not unlike the now thoroughly untenable idea of the 'filter bubble' itself, perhaps.

Adamic, Lada A. and Natalie Glance. 2005. 'The Political Blogosphere and the 2004 US Election: Divided They Blog'. In *Proceedings of the 3rd International Workshop on Link Discovery (LinkKDD '05)*, edited by Jafar Adibi, Marko Grobelnik, Dunja Mladenic and Patrick Pantel, 36–43. New York: ACM. https://doi.org/10.1145/1134271.1134277.

Anspach, Nicolas M. 2017. 'The New Personal Influence: How Our Facebook Friends Influence the News We Read'. *Political Communication* 34 (4): 590–606. https://doi.org/10.1080/10584609.2017.1316329.

Ausserhofer, Julian and Axel Maireder. 2013. 'National Politics on Twitter: Structures and Topics of a Networked Public Sphere'. *Information, Communication & Society* 16 (3): 291–314. https://doi.org/10.1080/1369118X.2012.756050.

Bail, Christopher A., Lisa P. Argyle, Taylor W. Brown, John P. Bumpus, Haohan Chen, M.B. Fallin Hunzaker, Jaemin Lee, Marcus Mann, Friedolin Merhout and Alexander Volfovsky. 2018. 'Exposure to Opposing Views on Social Media Can Increase Political Polarization'. *Proceedings of the National Academy of Sciences* 115 (37): 9216–21. https://doi.org/10.1073/pnas.1804840115.

Barberá, Pablo, John T. Jost, Jonathan Nagler, Joshua A. Tucker and Richard Bonneau. 2015. 'Tweeting from Left to Right: Is Online Political Communication More than an Echo Chamber?' *Psychological Science* 26 (10): 1531–42. https://doi.org/10.1177/0956797615594620.

References

Batorski, Dominik and Ilona Grzywińska. 2018. 'Three Dimensions of the Public Sphere on Facebook'. *Information, Communication & Society* 21 (3): 356–74. https://doi.org/10.1080/1369118X.2017.1281329.

Beam, Michael A. and Gerald M. Kosicki. 2014. 'Personalized News Portals: Filtering Systems and Increased News Exposure'. *Journalism & Mass Communication Quarterly* 91 (1): 59–77. https://doi.org/10.1177/1077699013514411.

Beam, Michael A., Jeffrey T. Child, Myiah J. Hutchens and Jay D. Hmielowski. 2018a. 'Context Collapse and Privacy Management: Diversity in Facebook Friends Increases Online News Reading and Sharing'. *New Media & Society* 20 (7): 2296–314. https://doi.org/10.1177/1461444817714790.

Beam, Michael A., Myiah J. Hutchens and Jay D. Hmielowski. 2018b. 'Facebook News and (De)Polarization: Reinforcing Spirals in the 2016 US Election'. *Information, Communication & Society* 21 (7): 940–58. https://doi.org/10.1080/1369118X.2018.1444783.

Benkler, Yochai, Robert Faris, Hal Roberts and Ethan Zuckerman. 2017. 'Study: Breitbart-Led Right-Wing Media Ecosystem Altered Broader Media Agenda'. *Columbia Journalism Review*, 3 March. http://www.cjr.org/analysis/breitbart-media-trump-harvard-study.php.

Bessi, Alessandro. 2016. 'Personality Traits and Echo Chambers on Facebook'. *Computers in Human Behavior* 65: 319–24. https://doi.org/10.1016/j.chb.2016.08.016.

Boxell, Levi, Matthew Gentzkow and Jesse M. Shapiro. 2017. 'Greater Internet Use Is Not Associated with Faster Growth in Political Polarization among US Demographic Groups'. *Proceedings of the National Academy of Sciences* 114 (40): 10612–17. https://doi.org/10.1073/pnas.1706588114.

Bozdag, Engin and Jeroen van den Hoven. 2015. 'Breaking the Filter Bubble: Democracy and Design'. *Ethics and Information Technology* 17 (4): 249–65. https://doi.org/10.1007/s10676-015-9380-y.

References

Bradshaw, Paul. 2016. 'Don't Blame Facebook for Your Own Filter Bubble'. *Online Journalism Blog*, 28 June. https://onlinejournalism blog.com/2016/06/28/dont-blame-facebook-for-your-own-filter-bubble/.

Brundidge, Jennifer. 2010. 'Encountering 'Difference' in the Contemporary Public Sphere: The Contribution of the Internet to the Heterogeneity of Political Discussion Networks'. *Journal of Communication* 60 (4): 680–700. https://doi.org/10.1111/j.1460-2466.2010.01509.x.

Brunner, Katharina and Sabrina Ebitsch. 2017. 'Von AfD bis Linkspartei – so politisch ist Facebook'. *Süddeutsche Zeitung*, 2 May. https://www.sueddeutsche.de/politik/politik-auf-facebook-rechte-abschottung-ohne-filterblase-1.3470137.

Bruns, Axel. 2017. 'Echo Chamber? What Echo Chamber? Reviewing the Evidence'. Paper presented at Future of Journalism 2017. Cardiff, 15 September. http://snurb.info/files/2017/Echo%20Chamber. pdf.

Bruns, Axel. 2018. *Gatewatching and News Curation: Journalism, Social Media, and the Public Sphere*. New York: Peter Lang.

Bruns, Axel, Brenda Moon, Felix Münch and Troy Sadkowsky. 2017. 'The Australian Twittersphere in 2016: Mapping the Follower/Followee Network'. *Social Media + Society* 3 (4): 1–15. https://doi.org/10.1177/2056305117748162.

Chong, Miyoung. 2018. 'Analyzing Political Information Network of the US Partisan Public on Twitter'. In *iConference 2018: Transforming Digital Worlds*, edited by Gobinda Chowdhury, Julie McLeod, Val Gillet and Peter Willett, 453–63. Cham: Springer International Publishing. https://doi.org/10.1007/978-3-319-78105-1_50.

Coleman, Stephen. 2003. 'A Tale of Two Houses: The House of Commons, the *Big Brother* House and the People at Home'. *Parliamentary Affairs* 56: 733–58. https://doi.org/10.1093/pa/gsg113.

References

Colleoni, Elanor, Alessandro Rozza and Adam Arvidsson. 2014. 'Echo Chamber or Public Sphere? Predicting Political Orientation and Measuring Political Homophily in Twitter Using Big Data'. *Journal of Communication* 64: 317–32. https://doi.org/10.1111/jcom.12084.

Dubois, Elizabeth and Grant Blank. 2018a. 'The Echo Chamber Is Overstated: The Moderating Effect of Political Interest and Diverse Media'. *Information, Communication & Society* 21 (5): 729–45. https://doi.org/10.1080/1369118X.2018.1428656.

Dubois, Elizabeth and Grant Blank. 2018b. 'The Myth of the Echo Chamber'. *The Conversation*, 8 March. http://theconversation.com/the-myth-of-the-echo-chamber-92544.

Duggan, Maeve and Aaron Smith. 2016. 'The Political Environment on Social Media'. Washington, DC: Pew Research Center. http://assets.pewresearch.org/wp-content/uploads/sites/14/2016/10/24160747/PI_2016.10.25_Politics-and-Social-Media_FINAL.pdf.

Eisenhower, Dwight D. 1961. 'Farewell Radio and Television Address to the American People, January 17th, 1961'. Dwight D. Eisenhower Presidential Library. https://www.eisenhower.archives.gov/all_about_ike/speeches/farewell_address.pdf.

Fletcher, Richard and Rasmus Kleis Nielsen. 2017. 'Are News Audiences Increasingly Fragmented? A Cross-National Comparative Analysis of Cross-Platform News Audience Fragmentation and Duplication'. *Journal of Communication* 67 (4): 476–98. https://doi.org/10.1111/jcom.12315.

Fletcher, Richard and Rasmus Kleis Nielsen. 2018. 'Are People Incidentally Exposed to News on Social Media? A Comparative Analysis'. *New Media & Society* 20 (7): 2450–68. https://doi.org/10.1177/1461444817724170.

Garimella, Kiran, Gianmarco De Francisci Morales, Aristides Gionis and Michael Mathioudakis. 2018. 'Political Discourse on Social Media: Echo Chambers, Gatekeepers, and the Price of Bipartisanship'. In *WWW'18 Proceedings of the 2018 World Wide Web Conference*,

913–22. Geneva: International World Wide Web Conferences Steering Committee. https://doi.org/10.1145/3178876.3186139.

Garrett, R. Kelly. 2009a. 'Echo Chambers Online? Politically Motivated Selective Exposure among Internet News Users'. *Journal of Computer-Mediated Communication* 14 (2): 265–85. https://doi.org/10.1111/j.1083-6101.2009.01440.x.

Garrett, R. Kelly. 2009b. 'Politically Motivated Reinforcement Seeking: Reframing the Selective Exposure Debate'. *Journal of Communication* 59 (4): 676–99. https://doi.org/10.1111/j.1460-2466.2009.01452.x.

Garrett, R. Kelly, Dustin Carnahan and Emily K. Lynch. 2013. 'A Turn toward Avoidance? Selective Exposure to Online Political Information, 2004–2008'. *Political Behavior* 35 (1): 113–34. https://doi.org/10.1007/s11109-011-9185-6.

Gentzkow, Matthew and Jesse M. Shapiro. 2011. 'Ideological Segregation Online and Offline'. *The Quarterly Journal of Economics* 126: 1799–839. https://doi.org/10.1093/qje/qjr044.

Graham, Tim and Robert Ackland. 2017. 'Do Socialbots Dream of Popping the Filter Bubble? The Role of Socialbots in Promoting Deliberative Democracy in Social Media'. In *Socialbots and Their Friends: Digital Media and the Automation of Sociality*, edited by Robert W. Gehl and Maria Bakardjieva, 187–206. New York: Routledge. https://www.taylorfrancis.com/books/c/9781317267393/chapters/10.4324%2F9781315637228-18.

Groshek, Jacob and Karolina Koc-Michalska. 2017. 'Helping Populism Win? Social Media Use, Filter Bubbles, and Support for Populist Presidential Candidates in the 2016 US Election Campaign'. *Information, Communication & Society* 20 (9): 1389–407. https://doi.org/10.1080/1369118X.2017.1329334.

Guess, Andrew M. 2016. 'Media Choice and Moderation: Evidence from Online Tracking Data'. Unpublished manuscript. New York University.

References

Guess, Andrew, Brendan Nyhan and Jason Reifler. 2018. 'Selective Exposure to Misinformation: Evidence from the Consumption of Fake News during the 2016 US Presidential Campaign'. Hanover, NH: Dartmouth College. http://www.dartmouth.edu/~nyhan/fake-news-2016.pdf.

Haim, Mario, Andreas Graefe and Hans-Bernd Brosius. 2018. 'Burst of the Filter Bubble? Effects of Personalization on the Diversity of Google News'. *Digital Journalism* 6 (3): 330–43. https://doi.org/10.1080/21670811.2017.1338145.

Helberger, Natali. 2011. 'Diversity by Design'. *Journal of Information Policy* 1: 441–69. https://doi.org/10.5325/jinfopoli.1.2011.0441.

Helberger, Natali. 2018. 'Challenging Diversity – Social Media Platforms and a New Conception of Media Diversity'. In *Digital Dominance: The Power of Google, Amazon, Facebook, and Apple*, edited by Martin Moore and Damian Tambini, 153–75. New York: Oxford University Press.

Hermida, Alfred. 2010. 'From TV to Twitter: How Ambient News Became Ambient Journalism'. *M/C Journal* 13 (2). http://journal.media-culture.org.au/index.php/mcjournal/article/view/220.

Katz, Elihu. 1996. 'And Deliver Us from Segmentation'. *The Annals of the American Academy of Political and Social Science* 546 (1): 22–33. https://doi.org/10.1177/0002716296546001003.

Katz, Elihu and Paul F. Lazarsfeld. 1955. *Personal Influence: The Part Played by People in the Flow of Mass Communications*. New York: Free Press.

Koene, Ansgar. 2016. 'Facebook's Algorithms Give It More Editorial Responsibility – Not Less'. *The Conversation*, 14 September. http://theconversation.com/facebooks-algorithms-give-it-more-editorial-responsibility-not-less-65182.

Krafft, Tobias D., Michael Gamer and Katharina A. Zweig. 2018. *Wer sieht was? Personalisierung, Regionalisierung und die Frage nach der Filterblase in Googles Suchmaschine*. Kaiserslautern: Algorithm

Watch. https://www.blm.de/files/pdf2/bericht-datenspende---wer-sieht-was-auf-google.pdf.

Krämer, Benjamin. 2017. 'Populist Online Practices: The Function of the Internet in Right-Wing Populism'. *Information, Communication & Society* 20 (9): 1293–309. https://doi.org/10.1080/13691 18X.2017.1328520.

Madsen, Anders Koed. 2016. 'Beyond the Bubble: Three Empirical Reasons for Re-Conceptualizing Online Visibility'. *MedieKultur: Journal of Media and Communication Research*, 31 (59): 6–27. https://doi.org/10.7146/mediekultur.v31i59.19235.

Marwick, Alice E. and danah boyd. 2011. 'I Tweet Honestly, I Tweet Passionately: Twitter Users, Context Collapse, and the Imagined Audience'. *New Media & Society* 13 (1): 114–33. https://doi.org/10. 1177/1461444810365313.

Meineck, Sebastian. 2018. 'Deshalb ist "Filterblase" die blödeste Metapher des Internets'. *Motherboard*, 9 March. https://motherboard. vice.com/de/article/pam5nz/deshalb-ist-filterblase-die-blodeste-metapher-des-internets.

Messing, Solomon and Sean J. Westwood. 2014. 'Selective Exposure in the Age of Social Media: Endorsements Trump Partisan Source Affiliation When Selecting News Online'. *Communication Research* 41 (8): 1042–63. https://doi.org/10.1177/0093650212466406.

Mitchell, Amy, Jeffrey Gottfried, Michael Barthel and Elisa Shearer. 2016. 'The Modern News Consumer: News Attitudes and Practices in the Digital Era'. Washington, DC: Pew Research Center. http:// www.journalism.org/2016/07/07/the-modern-news-consumer/.

Nechushtai, Efrat and Seth C. Lewis. 2019. 'What Kind of News Gatekeepers Do We Want Machines to Be? Filter Bubbles, Fragmentation, and the Normative Dimensions of Algorithmic Recommendations'. *Computers in Human Behavior*, 90: 298–307. https://doi.org/10.1016/j.chb.2018.07.043.

Negroponte, Nicholas. 1995. *Being Digital*. New York: Vintage.

References

Newman, Nic, David A.L. Levy and Rasmus Kleis Nielsen. 2015. *Reuters Institute Digital News Report 2015*. Oxford: Reuters Institute for the Study of Journalism, University of Oxford. https://reuters institute.politics.ox.ac.uk/our-research/digital-news-report-2015-0.

Newman, Nic, Richard Fletcher, David A.L. Levy and Rasmus Kleis Nielsen. 2016. *Reuters Institute Digital News Report 2016*. Oxford: Reuters Institute for the Study of Journalism, University of Oxford. https://reutersinstitute.politics.ox.ac.uk/our-research/digital-news-report-2016.

Nielsen, Rasmus Kleis. 2016. 'People Want Personalised Recommendations (Even as They Worry about the Consequences)'. In *Reuters Institute Digital News Report 2016*, by Nic Newman, Richard Fletcher, David A.L. Levy and Rasmus Kleis Nielsen, 112–14. Oxford: Reuters Institute for the Study of Journalism, University of Oxford. https://reutersinstitute.politics.ox.ac.uk/our-research/digital-news-report-2016.

Noelle-Neumann, Elisabeth. 1974. 'The Spiral of Silence: A Theory of Public Opinion'. *Journal of Communication* 24 (2): 43–51. https://doi.org/10.1111/j.1460-2466.1974.tb00367.x.

Nuernbergk, Christian. 2016. 'Political Journalists' Interaction Networks: The German Federal Press Conference on Twitter'. *Journalism Practice* 10 (7): 868–79. https://doi.org/10.1080/1751 2786.2016.1162669.

Obama, Barack. 2017. 'President Obama's Farewell Address: Full Video and Text'. *New York Times*, 10 January. https://www.nytimes. com/2017/01/10/us/politics/obama-farewell-address-speech.html.

O'Hara, Kieron. 2014. 'In Worship of an Echo'. *IEEE Internet Computing* 18 (4): 79–83. https://doi.org/10.1109/MIC.2014.71.

O'Hara, Kieron and David Stevens. 2015. 'Echo Chambers and Online Radicalism: Assessing the Internet's Complicity in Violent Extremism'. *Policy & Internet* 7 (4): 401–22. https://doi. org/10.1002/poi3.88.

References

Pariser, Eli. 2011. *The Filter Bubble: What the Internet Is Hiding from You*. London: Penguin.

Pariser, Eli. 2015. 'Did Facebook's Big Study Kill My Filter Bubble Thesis?' *Wired*, 7 May. https://www.wired.com/2015/05/did-facebooks-big-study-kill-my-filter-bubble-thesis/.

Quattrociocchi, Walter, Antonio Scala and Cass R. Sunstein. 2016. 'Echo Chambers on Facebook'. https://papers.ssrn.com/abstract=2795110.

Rietzschel, Antonie. 2017. 'Wie es in Facebooks Echokammern aussieht – von links bis rechts'. *Süddeutsche Zeitung*, 11 July. https://www.sueddeutsche.de/politik/mein-facebook-dein-facebook-wie-es-in-den-echokammern-von-links-bis-rechts-aussieht-1.3576513.

Schmidt, Jan-Hinrik, Lisa Merten, Uwe Hasebrink, Isabelle Petrich and Amelie Rolfs. 2017. 'Zur Relevanz von Online-Intermediären für die Meinungsbildung'. *Arbeitspapiere des Hans-Bredow-Instituts* 40. Hamburg: Hans-Bredow-Institut. https://www.hans-bredow-institut.de/uploads/media/default/cms/media/67256764e92e34539343a8c77a0215bd96b35823.pdf.

Sleeper, Manya, Rebecca Balebako, Sauvik Das, Amber Lynn McConahy, Jason Wiese and Lorrie Faith Cranor. 2013. 'The Post That Wasn't: Exploring Self-Censorship on Facebook'. In *Proceedings of the 2013 Conference on Computer-Supported Cooperative Work*, 793–802. New York: ACM. https://doi.org/10.1145/2441776.2441865.

Smith, Marc A., Lee Rainie, Itai Himelboim and Ben Shneiderman. 2014. 'Mapping Twitter Topic Networks: From Polarized Crowds to Community Clusters'. Washington, DC: Pew Research Center. http://www.pewresearch.org/wp-content/uploads/sites/9/2014/02/PIP_Mapping-Twitter-networks_022014.pdf.

Smith, Naomi and Tim Graham. 2017. 'Mapping the Anti-Vaccination Movement on Facebook'. *Information, Communication & Society*. https://doi.org/10.1080/1369118X.2017.1418406.

References

Spohr, Dominic. 2017. 'Fake News and Ideological Polarization: Filter Bubbles and Selective Exposure on Social Media'. *Business Information Review* 34 (3): 150–60. https://doi.org/10.1177/0266382117722446.

Starbird, Kate. 2017a. 'Information Wars: A Window into the Alternative Media Ecosystem'. *Medium*, 15 March. https://medium.com/hci-design-at-uw/information-wars-a-window-into-the-alternative-media-ecosystem-a1347f32fd8f.

Starbird, Kate. 2017b. 'Examining the Alternative Media Ecosystem through the Production of Alternative Narratives of Mass Shooting Events on Twitter'. In *11th International AAAI Conference on Web and Social Media*. Montréal: AAAI Press. http://faculty.washington.edu/kstarbi/Alt_Narratives_ICWSM17-CameraReady.pdf.

Sunstein, Cass R. 2001a. *Echo Chambers: Bush v. Gore, Impeachment, and Beyond*. Princeton, NJ: Princeton University Press.

Sunstein, Cass R. 2001b. *Republic.com*. Princeton, NJ: Princeton University Press.

Sunstein, Cass R. 2009. *Republic.com 2.0*. Princeton, NJ: Princeton University Press.

Sunstein, Cass R. 2017. *#Republic: Divided Democracy in the Age of Social Media*. Princeton, NJ: Princeton University Press.

Thorson, Kjerstin and Chris Wells. 2016. 'Curated Flows: A Framework for Mapping Media Exposure in the Digital Age'. *Communication Theory* 26 (3): 309–28. https://doi.org/10.1111/comt.12087.

Vaccari, Cristian, Augusto Valeriani, Pablo Barberà, John T. Jost, Jonathan Nagler and Joshua A. Tucker. 2016. 'Of Echo Chambers and Contrarian Clubs: Exposure to Political Disagreement among German and Italian Users of Twitter'. *Social Media + Society*. https://doi.org/10.1177/2056305116664221.

Valeriani, Augusto and Cristian Vaccari. 2016. 'Accidental Exposure to Politics on Social Media as Online Participation Equalizer in

Germany, Italy, and the United Kingdom'. *New Media & Society* 18 (9): 1857–74. https://doi.org/10.1177/1461444815616223.

Vriens, Eva and Erik van Ingen. 2018. 'Does the Rise of the Internet Bring Erosion of Strong Ties? Analyses of Social Media Use and Changes in Core Discussion Networks'. *New Media & Society* 20 (7): 2432–49. https://doi.org/10.1177/146144481772 4169.

Weeks, Brian E., Thomas B. Ksiazek and R. Lance Holbert. 2016. 'Partisan Enclaves or Shared Media Experiences? A Network Approach to Understanding Citizens' Political News Environments'. *Journal of Broadcasting & Electronic Media* 60 (2): 248–68. https://doi.org/10.1080/08838151.2016.1164170.

Weinberger, David. 2004. 'Is There an Echo in Here?' *Salon*, 21 February. https://www.salon.com/2004/02/21/echo_chamber/.

Weinberger, David. 2017. 'Pointing at the Wrong Villain: Cass Sunstein and Echo Chambers'. *Los Angeles Review of Books*, 20 July. https://lareviewofbooks.org/article/pointing-at-the-wrong-villain-cass-sunstein-and-echo-chambers/.

Williams, Hywel T.P., James R. McMurray, Tim Kurz and F. Hugo Lambert. 2015. 'Network Analysis Reveals Open Forums and Echo Chambers in Social Media Discussions of Climate Change'. *Global Environmental Change* 32: 126–38. https://doi.org/10.1016/j.gloenvcha.2015.03.006.

Wojcieszak, Magdalena E. and Diana C. Mutz. 2009. 'Online Groups and Political Discourse: Do Online Discussion Spaces Facilitate Exposure to Political Disagreement?' *Journal of Communication* 59 (1): 40–56. https://doi.org/10.1111/j.1460-2466.2008.01403.x.

Woolley, Samuel C. and Philip N. Howard. 2017. 'Computational Propaganda Worldwide: Executive Summary'. Working Paper 2017.11. Oxford: Computational Propaganda Research Project. http://comprop.oii.ox.ac.uk/wp-content/uploads/sites/89/2017/06/Case studies-ExecutiveSummary.pdf.

References

Wu, Shaomei, Jake M. Hofman, Winter A. Mason and Duncan J. Watts. 2011. 'Who Says What to Whom on Twitter'. In *Proceedings of the 20th International Conference on World Wide Web (WWW 2011)*, 705–14. New York: ACM. https://doi.org/10.1145/1963405.1963504.

Yang, Shuzhe, Anabel Quan-Haase and Kai Rannenberg. 2017. 'The Changing Public Sphere on Twitter: Network Structure, Elites and Topics of the #righttobeforgotten'. *New Media & Society* 19 (12): 1983–2002. https://doi.org/10.1177/1461444816651409.

Yardi, Sarita and danah boyd. 2010. 'Dynamic Debates: An Analysis of Group Polarization over Time on Twitter'. *Bulletin of Science, Technology & Society* 30 (5): 316–27. https://doi.org/10.1177/0270467610380011.

Zuiderveen Borgesius, Frederik J., Damian Trilling, Judith Möller, Balázs Bodó, Claes H. de Vreese and Natali Helberger. 2016. 'Should We Worry about Filter Bubbles?' *Internet Policy Review* 5 (1). https://doi.org/10.14763/2016.1.401.

Index

Index

Index

Index

Index